52-Charlie

Members of a Legendary Pilot Training Class Share Their Stories about Combat in Korea and Vietnam

Edward T. Gushee

52-Charlie: Members of a Legendary Pilot Training Class Share Their Stories about Combat in Korea and Vietnam

Published by Wheatmark®
610 East Delano Street, Suite 104
Tucson, Arizona 85705 U.S.A.
www.wheatmark.com

Publisher's Cataloging-In-Publication Data

Gushee, Edward T.

52-Charlie : members of a legendary pilot training class share their stories about combat in Korea and Vietnam / Edward T. Gushee.

p. : ill. ; cm.

ISBN: 978-1-60494-204-0

1. United States. Air Force--History. 2. Korean War, 1950-1953--Aerial operations, American--Personal narratives, American. 3. Vietnam War, 1961-1975--Aerial operations, American--Personal narratives, American. 4. Fighter pilots--United States. 5. Fighter planes--United States--History. I. Title. II. Title: Fifty-two Charlie : members of a legendary pilot training class share their stories about combat in Korea and Vietnam

E840.4.G8 2009
973.92 2008942613

Dedication

This book is dedicated to all those men and women who have served their country in the armed forces and especially those who graduated in the Aviation Cadet Class of 52-Charlie. As a class we particularly honor those members who died in the skies over Korea and Vietnam as well as those who have since joined the Honor Flight of 52-C.

They are the true heroes of our generation.

While you read 52-CHARLIE say a quiet thank you to those who currently serve our country so bravely and so selflessly.

They are the true heroes of today's generation.

In Appreciation

We would like to thank Sears Holdings Corporation for continuing to support the men and women of our armed services. They have done so for many years, unselfishly, without recognition or fan fare, in good times and bad. This fine company has earned the gratitude of every single American as well as all of us who have had the honor of serving our country in times of peril.

Note to Reader

The pictures herein are more than fifty years old. They were not professional photographs to begin with. Time has taken its toll. In a sense, however, they tell a story that bright, shiny, perfect reproductions could never tell.

Contents

The Class of 52-Charlie

The moment a pilot lifts a plane off a runway for the first time, his or her life is changed forever. Nothing will ever match it. It is a strange mixture of unfettered freedom and indefinable excitement, tinged by unspoken risk. Yet that risk is very real. And when that pilot moves on to more complicated machinery, such as a fighter or a bomber, that risk becomes greater. Add to that enemy fire in combat and the risk mounts exponentially. Yet the excitement of flying, the freedom from restraints, the exhilaration of the moment wash away thoughts of danger. Combat pilots. Men and women. They are a strange lot, an extraordinary group who flirt with death and enjoy each moment of that very courtship.

This is a book about pilots who graduated in the aviation cadet class of 1952-Charlie, a class of more than four hundred pilots, most of whom flew combat in Korea and Vietnam. Many lost their lives in these wars and became the charter members of our Honor Flight. We honor those we lost and we will always remember them. And when our class finally reconvenes as a unit in the hereafter, oh, the stories we will have to tell!

The Korean War began on June 25, 1950, and lasted just over three years and one month. It was often referred to as a police action, not a war. As years pass, it has become the forgotten war. Yet in those three years over four million men, women, and children were killed or wounded. The United States alone suffered 54,000 dead and 103,000 wounded. Almost as many GIs were killed in Korea as were killed in the fourteen years of fighting in Vietnam.

The Vietnam War became the most unpopular war ever fought. It tore at the fabric of our very existence. It divided our country. Draft cards were destroyed. Our flag was publicly burned. Many of our young men moved to Canada to escape conscription. Soldiers, sailors, and airmen were spit upon for doing nothing more than offering to sacrifice their lives for their country. And during that awful time, many of my classmates were killed in the skies above Vietnam or in the prisons at Hanoi.

I am honored to have been a member of 52-Charlie. I am proud to have served. I am proud to be a part of a group who gave their skills and their lives to protect the people of South Korea and South Vietnam, people whom they had never met before and few have seen since.

The stories herein are stories of dedication, often humorous, sometimes tragic.

In the late 80s, a class member, Dick Spaulding, commissioned a painting of the training planes flown by members of 52-Charlie. The artist, Jack McCoy, included a Navy plane in the painting and entitled it *Bogie 3 O'clock*. The naval plane, a TBF Avenger, was the type flown by President George H. W. Bush, who inscribed the painting in the White House, "Congratulations to 52 Charlie class members."

The planes used in the training of 52-Charlie. F-86, B-25, F-80, F-51, T-33, and the AT-6. The Avenger is in the lower left.

President George H. W. Bush signs the painting in the White House with the artist Jack McCoy and Dick Spaulding.

Part One

Aviation Cadet Training

LEARNING TO FLY...THE AT-6

April 1, 1951: the class of 52-Charlie was assembled. More than four hundred cadets received orders to report to one of six primary training bases: Greenville and Columbus in Mississippi, Spence in Moultrie, Georgia, and Connelly, Goodfellow, and Perrin, all in Texas. Greenville, Connelly, and Spence were civilian contract bases. The Air Force didn't have enough instructor pilots to teach a class the size of 52-C, so they staffed three bases with retired WW II pilots. Most had combat experience, and after retiring from the service they continued to fly as instructors, crop dusters, or in some other semi-perilous activity where they could relive some of the excitement they experienced chasing enemy planes or strafing ground ordnance. They were crazy men but extraordinary pilots. And they were loved by their students.

The training plane used in primary was a WW II aircraft, the

The venerable AT-6, the plane most cadets soloed in. The AT-6 went to war in Korea as a spotter in the Mosquito Squadron.

AT-6, affectionately known as the T-6. It was a hot aircraft, with a 600-horsepower Pratt and Whitney 1340 radial engine capable of reaching a speed of more than two hundred knots and a ceiling of 23,000 feet. It was the perfect plane in which to learn aerobatics, but it had a shortcoming, a tendency to ground loop on landing.

I enlisted in Aviation Cadets the year I graduated from Williams College.

My orders took me to Greenville AFB, where I spent my first two weeks in ground school. There I learned every system in the T-6. I learned about isobars and anvils and thunderheads, high-pressure fronts and cold fronts and the jet stream. I learned the phonetic alphabet, and then because there were so many foreign students, Able, Baker, Charlie, became Alpha, Bravo, Cocoa, and I had a whole new phonetic alphabet to learn.

On the morning of the third week I donned my flight suit for the first time and went to the briefing room to meet my instructor pilot, Roy Hope, and my two flying partners, Ed Durnal and Ray Fausel.

Hope's group: Durnal, Gushee, Hope, Fausel. Our T-6s are in the background.

We drew straws to see who would be the first to fly with Hope. I won. I put on my parachute, had my picture taken, climbed into the front seat of my T-6, and fastened the shoulder harness. I was nervous and a bit concerned. Hope got in the back seat, closed the canopy, and taxied to the active runway, where he yelled through the mike, "Don't just sit there, take this goddamn plane off!"

I was too scared to ask, "How?" I pushed the throttle forward, guided the plane with the rudders, grabbed the stick with my right hand, and tried to choke it to death. Soon the plane lifted off the runway and my life changed forever.

First-day jitters

The fetters were released. There is an indescribable exhilaration the first time you take a plane off, a different world in the blue-and-white sky that you get to know only through the feeling of a control stick.

Hope took over and I began to wonder why I ever left home. He completed a few slow rolls, a barrel roll, a lazy eight, and a loop—at which point my stomach and I parted company. Hope was a touch crazier than most of the other instructor pilots. He made the T-6 do things it was never designed to do, and he expected as much from his three students. He demonstrated how he attacked German trains during WW II and when he wasn't flying below minimums, he was doing his damnedest to tear the elevators off the plane with his most-loved aerobatic maneuver, the hammerhead stall.

My earphones crackled and Hope told me he was going to show me how to enter a spin and, more importantly, how to get out of it. He added, "I am only going to show you one time so you goddamn well better pay attention."

And then it was my turn. That's when I saw the face of every cadet who failed to pull out of a spin. Sweat stained my flight suit and dripped down my wrists. I pulled the T-6 up and just before it stalled, I kicked right rudder and there it was, a spin. I wondered would I ever get out of it? Dip the nose, pick up speed, neutralize the controls, and soon I was flying straight and level.

By then it was time to return to the field. Hope had two other students to terrify. But I had succeeded. I put my plane into a spin and recovered without help from the back seat. My smile stretched forever, and there was nothing that wisecracking, crop-dusting fool could say to take it away.

While I was busy patting myself on the back, I heard a scream from the back seat, "The GUMP check you idiot! In case you haven't been listening in class, G is for gas, switch to the full tank. U is for undercarriage. It would be nice to lower the wheels before we land. M is for mixture. Put it on rich, we don't want the engine to quit on final approach and P is for propeller. High rpm."

Having completed the GUMP check, I entered the landing pattern on the downwind leg.

"Are you going to try and land this bird without flaps? If so, let me out now."

"But there is no F in GUMP," I complained.

"I'll tell you what the F stands for if you don't give me fifteen degrees."

Hope took over and landed the plane. All in all, it was one hell of a day.

During the next two weeks, I spent as much time in ground school as I did in the sky. A pilot who doesn't understand all the systems of the aircraft he is flying, who doesn't know about weather and cumulus-nimbus clouds, navigation and flight plans and restricted areas, and a thousand other things is a dead pilot.

I made a dozen landings at three thousand feet. A landing is nothing more than a controlled stall and before you practice that stall on the ground, you practice it in the air. But there was much more to learn. We spent hours doing aerobatics: lazy eights, slow rolls, loops, and spins. I spent an ungodly amount of time in inverted flight, looking at the world from the wrong side up, and all the time Hope screaming at me from the back seat, "Goddamn it, Gushee, that was shit, do it again!"

But the louder he yelled, the wider the smile on my face.

Once in a Lifetime

The day I soloed. The back seat is empty.

Three hours a day, six days a week for almost three weeks I listened to Hope yell instructions at me as I took off or landed or flew aerobatics. Then came that special day, the day I will never forget.

It began at an auxiliary field where I anticipated shooting several touch-and-go landings. That's the type of landing where the student pilot lands the plane and while still rolling down the runway pushes the throttles forward to take off again. The auxiliary field did not have a control tower, only a radio shack manned by a controller.

I touched down and was about to put the power back on when Hope yelled, "What the hell are you doing?"

"A touch-and-go!"

"The hell you are! Taxi over to the tarmac and let me out of this thing. I can't stand flying with you for a minute longer."

When we reached the tarmac, Hope popped the canopy and got out. Walking away from the aircraft, he shouted over his shoulder, "Make three takeoffs and three landings, then if you're still alive, pick me up."

That was my special day! The day I soloed.

I lined up for my first solo takeoff, my feet on the brakes, my heart in my mouth. Control called my number and cleared me for takeoff. As I gathered speed down the runway I remember how quiet it was. The engine roared, but there wasn't a sound coming from the rear seat. I had a smile on my face that barely fit in the cockpit.

It is generally assumed that the most exciting moment in one's life is when you get married or when your first child is born. Add to that the day you solo, the first time you take a plane off the ground, fly it around the field, and land it without an instructor in the back seat.

There wasn't a single part of my body that didn't tingle. There wasn't anyone so deaf that they couldn't hear my shouts of joy above the roar of the radial engine. There wasn't a time in my life of which I was prouder than the moment my T-6 gently lifted off the runway that April morning. The whole sky belonged to me and me alone.

Control cleared me in for my first solo landing. I knew Hope was watching and I was going to make damn sure my landing was perfect. And it was! God was I proud! Even that acerbic SOB would have to admit it was pretty good.

The second takeoff and landing also went well. But I forgot one important thing that April morning. I forgot I was flying with a group of college-age cadets who loved to one-up their fellow pilots. The opportunity availed itself when the tower radio failed. The only voice transmissions after that came from other cadets in the pattern. I had just turned onto final approach for my final landing when my radio screamed at me, "Plane on final approach, your gear is down! Your gear is down!"

My heart swallowed the rest of me. I was about to land my T-6 with the gear up. I was about to crash on my first day of soloing. I did the only thing possible, I poured the coal to the T-6 and took it around. Just as I did, I realized I'd been had. The transmission said that my gear was down. Of course it was down because that's the way it's supposed to be when you land. My face was Ferrari red and I knew instantly who the perpetrator was. It was Chappy McDonnell. Chappy had a wit the size of his flying skills, which were awesome, and he was not averse to using it.

Now I had to pick up Hope. "What the hell was that all about? Why did you take it around?"

I made some feeble excuse, which Hope didn't buy. But I didn't care. I had just soloed and nothing would ever replace the memory of that moment.

There's Nothing So Black as a Moonlit Night

There were times when things didn't always go the way I wanted, such as when I made a lousy landing or didn't complete an aerobatic maneuver correctly. There were also moments of exaltation. One came on an exercise called "stages," when each cadet was required to make six power-off landings and six takeoffs while a group of instructors sat in judgment. The best score possible for a landing and a takeoff was one. The best score for all six was six. If you missed your touchdown spot by more than a couple of feet, a point was added to your score. If you didn't land in a perfect three-point position, a point was added. If you added power on the final approach, a couple of extra points came your way. If your takeoff roll was erratic, two points were added and so on.

I completed the stage with a score of seven points and was certain that it was a cadet record. I'd just given Hope bragging rights for a month against his closest friend, Lonnie McGee. Unfortunately, McGee's student, and my best friend, Jim Griffith, had scored the impossible six. Fifty-six years later, Jim Griffith reminds me about his six every chance he gets, and he makes sure those chances come often.

The two instructor pilots decided to close ranks and lord it over every other IP on the base. They were impossible. Each won a case of beer, which they shared with their students. It was such an extraordinary moment that I think Hope came close to saying something civil to me. I saw it in his eyes that day, but it passed quickly.

Our training intensified and ground school became more demanding. We had less than six weeks to graduation and the commanding officer of the base was determined that the cadets he sent to advanced were the best-trained student pilots in the Air Force. It wasn't enough to just complete an aerobatic maneuver; precision was required. A loop had to be a perfect loop. A roll had to be precise, a lazy-eight symmetric. An Immelman righted at the apex, inverted flight straight and level and Hope made damn sure the colonel's wishes were carried out to the letter.

The stricter Hope became, the more I enjoyed it. We were now proficient in daylight flying. Now it was time to learn how to fly at night. We began each morning in ground school before flying several hours in the afternoon. Following dinner we returned to the flight line for three hours of night flying.

Hope guided me through my first three night landings. After that he watched from the ground as I completed my night requirements in preparation for my cross-country flight to Memphis. My takeoff was normal. I climbed to my assigned altitude where I could make out the city lights of Memphis. I aimed the plane at the lights and let the engine do the rest. Once I reached Memphis, I gained a thousand feet; turned 180 degrees, and headed back to the base. I was so confident that I threw my map into the rear seat, sat back, smoked a cigarette, and headed for home.

But God was in a sporty mood that night. He ordered a wind shift at the new altitude, so simply turning 180 degrees and flying a reciprocal heading wasn't going to work.

Unlike Memphis, the lights at Greenville consisted of a twenty-five-watt bulb at Doe's Eat Place, a few candles at the Greenville yacht club, and a small fire under a moonshiner's vat. Despite the full moon, I never saw such darkness in my life. I flew the required time, but the beacon at the airbase was nowhere to be seen. I dropped down to a thousand feet and searched patiently for the Mississippi River that would guide me back to the base. I was sure I could find the largest river in the United States at night. I crisscrossed the terrain below. I dove. I turned on my landing lights, but I could find no river. You can't miss seeing the Mississippi River on a moonlit night, can you? Apparently you can.

I was lost. And being lost in the air with limited fuel is not quite the same as being lost on the ground. I had already been in the air twenty minutes longer than scheduled. I switched back and forth from one fuel tank to the other, watching as the fuel gauges dropped ever lower. I looked for a lighted highway or even a flat piece of ground on which I might make an emergency landing. I even considered the possibility of bailing out.

Another twenty minutes passed. I considered breaking radio silence and calling a Mayday, when off in the distance I saw a friendly green-and-white beacon light. It was home!

My flight suit was soaked with perspiration as I prepared for landing. I knew Hope would be there to meet me so I braced myself for the invective that was sure to follow. But surprisingly, there was a hint of a smile on his face. His lips turned up at the ends. As I pulled back the canopy, he slapped me on the back and said, "Goddamn it, I knew it! You're the smartest student I have. You stayed up long enough to finish all your night solo requirements. My other two dunces got back here on time, so I gotta give up another evening while they complete their night requirements. That pisses me off!"

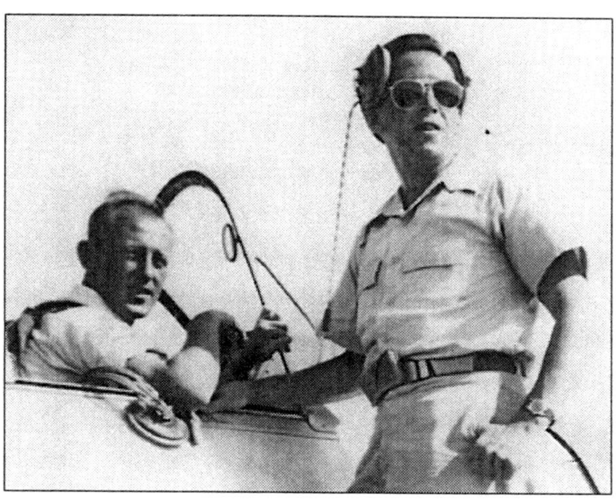

Griffith and Gushee's instructors: McGee and Hope. Two of the best.

Anyone out There Know Where the Hell I Am?

The cross-country flight back to Vance was a bit more than Joe Ortega bargained for.

I was not the only cadet to get lost on a cross-country flight. Joe Ortega met his Mississippi River on a day/night cross-country flight from Enid, Oklahoma. The day part of his flight took Ortega to Kansas City, where he was to refuel and complete his night requirements by returning to Enid. However, the base in Kansas City was out of T-6 fuel. Ortega did the math and realized he had enough gas to get back to Vance but not a lot more.

He took off and ran into a squall line a short time later. His T-6 was all over the sky. He was low on fuel and had no idea where he was. One tank was almost empty. The other registered less than a quarter of a tank. Ortega called Wichita and asked for a direction-finder steer to Vance and was told that all the DF operators were in Texas on temporary duty.

Joe didn't know it, but he was over Norwich, Kansas. He had two options: climb until the engine stopped and bail out or buzz the town in the hope someone might take notice and call Vance. A retired Air Force P-51 pilot chairing a meeting about sewage with the local townspeople heard Ortega's plane and sensed he was in trouble. He asked the group to follow him.

They drove their cars to a wheat field and lined up in such a way that their lights outlined a makeshift landing strip. At one end they parked a car, which Ortega assumed was the beginning of the strip.

But it wasn't his night.

Instead of marking the touchdown spot it marked the end of the runway, where a dense stand of tall trees began. Ortega switched on his landing lights and lowered his flaps, but he wisely did not put down his gear. He intended to make a belly landing.

As he was about to touch down, he saw trees staring him in the face. He pushed his throttles forward and prayed to God that he had enough fuel to top the trees. He did and landed safely on the other side in a field. His prop and flaps were badly damaged and his pride was at an all-time low.

When Ortega returned to his base, his friends had put out the welcome sign and they never let him forget his unusual landing in a Kansas wheat field.

The T-6 looked worse than it was. The next day Vance sent out a truck, a maintenance crew, and a photographer to pick up the T-6. Both fuel tanks were empty. But Ortega had made a fine belly landing and the T-6 was back in the air within three days,

Ortega and I were not the only ones who messed up a cross-county trip. Jake Reider won the prize for getting lost over one of the world's most identifiable visual sightings in broad daylight. Jake flew

It's nice to know someone cares. Yeah!

his T-28 out of Bryan AFB and somewhere along the line his map, ground sightings, compass, and judgment came to a crossroad. He had no idea where he was and the sun was about to go down. Reider called for help. He was asked to give a visual sighting.

"Well, there is a big lake ahead and I am near an airfield where there's a lot of activity."

"Roger, give us a short count."

Jake the Lake Reider. He had his own Mississippi River.

Jake counted slowly backwards from five and waited patiently until triangulation could pinpoint his position.

"T-28, this is Ellington AFB and we are right below you. You've been instructed to land here."

"Roger, Ellington. I will report in on downwind."

"By the way, you know that lake you saw?"

"What about it, tower?"

"Well, we have a name for that little old lake. We call it the Gulf of Mexico."

Missing the Mississippi River at night is one thing, confusing the Gulf of Mexico for a lake is yet another. Reider landed at Ellington and an instructor pilot from his base flew down to pick him up. On his return to Bryan, Reider found a large sign on a 35-gallon barrel with the inscription, "Welcome home, Jake the Lake." Behind the barrel was a map with "Gulf of Mexico" lined out, and in large letters, "Jake's Lake" inked in.

Reider's thrills were just beginning, as were Ortega's. Korea awaited them.

Glen Wampler and His Ronson Lighter

Cadet Wampler is awarded a plaque for "Outstanding Cadet." This had to be before Truax and NOTAMS.

Some cadets were simply destined to create havoc. While Ortega and Jake the Lake and I did it with our navigational skills, Glen Wampler did it with his Ronson lighter. Glen spent most of his flying career saying, "Thank God," "Whew," and "How'd I miss that?"

Wampler had gone through primary training with Joe Ortega at Spence Field in Georgia. One morning Glen was practicing aerobatics at five thousand feet in his T-6 when sparks and flames erupted under the instrument panel. He took off his garrison cap and started beating the flames. When that didn't work, he knew he might have to bail out as the whole damn plane could blow up. He opened the canopy to jump, but that fanned the flames and literally engulfed him, so he slammed the canopy shut.

Wampler realized the sparks had to be from an electrical short, so he switched off the battery, which stopped the sparks. He continued fighting the fire with his cap until the flames died.

When Wampler landed, he was chagrined to find the source of the problem. At some point during his flight, his Ronson lighter had fallen out of his pocket and wedged into the wiring, shorting a couple of wires. The lighter fluid did the rest and burned an inch-long hole in Wampler's beloved lighter.

Glen's Ronson lighter fifty years later, Glen blamed it on the Air Force for designing flying suits without zippers.

This was only the beginning for Lieutenant Wampler. He was an accident waiting to happen. During gunnery competition in Yuma, Arizona, he failed to position his plane properly behind a target being towed by another plane. In order to correct it, he over-controlled his F-86, which caused it to snap roll. Wampler blacked out; his plane nosed over and headed towards the ground. By the time he regained consciousness, he was so close to the ground that he could count the individual blades of grass. He managed to level his plane off and return to base to await the next chapter in the Perils of Glen Wampler.

Wampler didn't have long to wait. While stationed in Sault Ste. Marie in northern Michigan, Wampler was asked to fly an F-86D with an inoperative hydraulic system to Truax in Madison, Michigan, for mechanical work. Without hydraulics, a jet is difficult to fly and even more difficult to land. Imagine driving an 18-wheel truck without power steering or trying to stop it without power brakes and then multiply that by a factor of ten.

But Wampler wasn't concerned. The runway at Truax is more than 10,000-feet long, more than enough concrete to stop his aircraft without hydraulics.

But—Wampler made one small mistake. He forgot to check the NOTAMS at Truax before taking off. (NOTAMS are published by every Air Force base to advise pilots of any unusual conditions that exist at that airfield).

As he approached Truax, Wampler called the tower for landing instructions and was told that the 10,000-foot runway was closed for repairs. The runway he was assigned was only 5,200 feet long. He didn't have enough fuel to fly to an alternate base, but he wasn't overly concerned. The F-86 has a spare single-shot hydraulic system for use in an emergency. Wampler could use that shot to activate the speed brakes to lower his landing speed. The 86 is also equipped with a drag chute. He approached the runway just above stalling speed, touched down, hit the speed brakes, and deployed the drag chute.

The drag chute pulled away from the plane and fell to the ground. Someone hadn't attached it properly. Fifty-two hundred feet of runway flashed under his plane as Wampler headed toward a state highway, clogged with traffic. He climbed on the manual brakes with every ounce of his strength, his legs screaming in pain. Wampler was certain he would join the traffic as soon as he broke through the fence separating the field from the road.

Rubber burned, tires screamed; the plane slowed down and finally came to rest two feet short of the fence, while drivers on the road stared bug-eyed at the smoking plane. Wampler's legs hurt so much he had to call for help to get out of the cockpit.

Glen Wampler tested God's will at every turn, and God must have had a good laugh.

On to Advanced

The cadet program consists of six months of basic and six months of advanced training. Each cadet was initially given the option of finishing his training program in single-engine or multi-engine aircraft. Those scheduled for multi-engines were sent to Vance in Oklahoma or Reese in Texas. Single-engine jocks went to Bryan in Texas, Craig in Alabama, or Williams in Arizona. After my night cross-country experience I opted for multi-engine school, where I would be flying with a navigator. I didn't want to spend my entire Air Force career looking for the Mississippi River. I was posted to Vance.

All things have a way of changing in the military. Their needs dictate those changes. When we arrived at Vance, we were told that there was a greater need for fighter pilots in Korea than bomber pilots, so all but thirty cadets at Vance were transferred to single engines. Names were drawn from a hat and I was one of the thirty who would continue in the multi-engine program.

I spent the next six months flying the Billy Mitchell bomber, the B-25, an easily recognizable plane with twin engines and twin vertical stabilizers. Its powerful Wright Cyclone engines framed the glass-house cockpit. It bristled with five 50-caliber guns and had a ceiling of 25,000 feet. Jimmy Doolittle and his group of pilots flew B-25s off a carrier in 1942 and became the first Americans to bomb Tokyo. It is a comfortable airplane and can fly as confidently at a hundred feet as it does at ten thousand. But the sound of its Cyclone engines could take an eardrum in no time. When we flew, we kept our earphones on both ears.

Some of the thirty chosen ones: From the left: Doran, Krag, Prather, Griffith, Diddle, Gordon, Shannon, Miller, Beck, Rothleitner,

Dombaugh, Carlson, Michaletz
The B-25, one of the best planes ever built. Forgiving and a ton of fun.

Jim Griffith and I were flying partners and roommates. Aerobatics were now a thing of the past, but some new wrinkles were added to our curriculum, formation and instrument flying. My instructor pilot, Lieutenant Lepic, would place a special plastic shield over the windscreen and hand me a pair of colored glasses to wear. I could see the instruments clearly, but I could not see out of the airplane. Lepic asked me to close my eyes and then put the 25 through a series of maneuvers designed to confuse the hell out of my inner ear.

"It's your plane," Lepic announced, "take over."

I was certain we were inverted and the first thing I tried to do was to turn the plane right side up.

"Look at your goddamn instruments, Gushee! Don't listen to your ear. Its wrong! Look!"

The instruments told a different story. The plane was straight and level. The pilot who doesn't trust his instruments is a dead pilot. Before any cadet graduates from advanced training he must earn an in-

Cadet Gushee just prior to his cross-country trip to Hollywood.

strument card and be able to fly his plane in situations where he can't see five feet outside the cockpit.

The training was intense, but there were some wonderful moments, many of which were spent in the cadet bar. We did not fly on Sunday, so Saturday night was a night of debauchery. On Sunday morning the 25s were filled with cadets sucking on the oxygen system, doing their damnedest to cure their hangovers.

My days of screaming at the sky while twisting my plane into an aerobatic pretzel were over, but there were compensations. The dreaded cross-country was now a friend. We no longer flew solo. Every flight carried a pilot and a co-pilot. Each flight team could schedule two cross-county missions to destinations of their choosing. Griffith and I chose to go to Hollywood on one of our cross-country trips because my godfather was a close friend of Walt Disney and could arrange a VIP tour of a studio.

Our flight took us to Los Angeles by way of Denver. We passed

Gregory Peck on the set of The Snows Of Kilamanjaro *with Lieutenant Lepic, Gushee, and Griffith.*

over the Rockies at night before landing in L.A. where we had a quick drink and went to bed. The next morning we met our guide in Beverly Hills. He drove us to Twentieth-Century Fox where they were filming *The Snows of Kilimanjaro* with Gregory Peck and Susan Hayward.

Just outside the shooting stage was a large trailer. As we were about to enter the stage, the trailer door opened and Susan Hayward smiled down on us. Miss Hayward was not only a beautiful and talented actress, she was also extremely gracious. Inside the studio, we were introduced to the director, Henry King, Gregory Peck, and other members of the cast. We watched the rest of the day, fascinated. When they wrapped, Mr. Peck invited us to join him and a few friends at the studio that evening to view a pre-release film entitled *The African Queen.*

What a night that was!

Jim Griffith decided that weekend that he was going to be a movie

Bill Payne and Jim Griffith pay their respects to a fallen classmate Cadet Gushee at the Last Frontier in Las Vegas.

actor. His wish was realized when he appeared some years later as a pilot in *Strategic Air Command* starring Jimmy Stewart.

My second cross-country took sixteen cadets to The Last Frontier in Vegas to appear in a photo shoot. Sixteen cadets and a host of beautiful chorus girls made this a weekend to remember. I didn't go to bed the first night we were there and because the light intensity in a casino never varies, I lost track of time and was late to the shoot the next morning. When I finally arrived there was little they could do with me. They placed me in a glass hearse with a drink on my chest and took a picture. I kept saying to myself, "I hope this is the only hearse I get into during my military career."

We returned to our base exhausted but with a B-25 full of memories. A few weeks later, we graduated from cadets and were given our wings and our second-lieutenant bars.

The B-29—Hero of the Past

The B-29 was the workhorse in the pacific during WW II. It dropped the atomic bomb on Hiroshima and Nagasaki. But it was an easy prey for the MiG -15 during daylight bombing raids in Korea.

We were no longer cadets, but our training had just begun. Some classmates were sent to Nellis or Luke to learn how to fly combat jets. Some were checked out in the F-51. Some were sent to Randolph AFB to fly the B-29. Others were assigned to the Military Air Transport Service. Most were preparing to fly combat in Southeast Asia. It was a sobering thought. The carefree days of the past year had drawn to a close. 52-Charlie was about to lose several of its best pilots in training and in combat.

Those of us who received orders to Randolph would spend the next six weeks learning every system in the B-29. Six weeks pulling that huge monster off the runway and shooting touch-and-gos, of learning how to land without flaps or with one or two engines feathered. Six weeks in a metal link trainer that raised the hackles on your neck when the instructor cranked a fire into your flight plan or caused a thunderstorm to welcome you to the runway, six weeks training in a high-altitude chamber where you were asked to take off your oxygen mask and play patty-cake with a partner until he could no longer coordinate his movements. Six weeks going through explosive decompression with its dense fog and ear-popping sensation; six weeks of concentrated training and flying that flew by with Mach 1 speed.

The moment those six weeks passed, I was sent to escape-and-evasion school at Stead AFB outside Reno, Nevada, to learn how to evade capture and live off the land should I be shot down behind enemy lines.

In two weeks at Stead, I learned how to make jerky and how to use a parachute to make shoes or a sleeping bag. I was told which bugs and animals I could eat and which ones to let go, which plants were nutritious and which ones would make me sick. I was taught how to rig for an air pickup and shown how short field landings and takeoffs were done with the use of JATO (jet-assisted-takeoff) bottles.

I had one week to digest a month's worth of materials and then what I learned was put into practice. We were divided up into crews of eleven, the same number that flew on a 29. Each crew was taken to the boonies, each man provided with a pouch that had everything an airman would find in his parachute were he to bail out over enemy territory. A destination some forty miles away was assigned, and we were given five days to complete the mission. Five days. That seemed pretty simple, but there was a wrinkle. The forty miles went through the mountains at Lake Tahoe and several hundred airmen were doing their utmost to capture you. If you were caught, you went through hell … interrogation and intimidation.

The interrogators' tactics were publicly questioned in later years. The fact that these tactics were designed to save your life in war was of little consequence. At Stead you knew you would not be maimed or killed, but as a prisoner of war in Asia that was not the case. The officers at Stead tried to prepare airmen for that eventuality. Their instruction, their words, helped several downed pilots escape and others avoid interrogation and the beatings that often followed.

Uncomfortable? You bet! Life threatening? No! Often a prisoner was forced to place his chin on a wall while his hands were tied behind his back and his feet placed well away from the wall. He was forced to stay that way until he fainted or fell. At times a prisoner had his shoes removed and was put outdoors in an open yard covered with broken glass so that he had to move very carefully or stay still while the October winds bit into him. This was done with the goal of proving that if you are caught behind enemy lines you are not going to get away with name, rank, and serial number.

The first day of the trek was a free day. An instructor guide accompanied each crew and demonstrated how to build fires that could not be seen, how to lay traps for rabbits, how to use a gill net in a stream, and how best to use the items in your pouch. These items included sugar cubes, dried coffee, tea, a honey bar, and a bar of pemmican—enough concentrated energy to see you through a week without any other sustenance.

There was a problem: In order to cover the forty miles to the meeting point no crew could stay in one place long enough to fish or hunt. You could exist on the honey bar, the sugar, and the pemmican for five days. The first day out I smelled the honey bar and the pemmican and decided that no matter how hungry I got, I would never eat that stuff, so I threw it away. It's strange the actions a full stomach can dictate. I would live on two lumps of sugar a day for the next five days.

The morning of the second day the instructors left and we were on our own, walking as carefully as we could and making certain that the enemy was nowhere to be seen. It didn't take long, though, for our urban crew to walk into an enemy camp. We fled in eight different directions. Nine were caught. Only Lieutenant Carlson and I managed to get away. We hid in a thick bush and watched as the enemy walked back and forth in front of us. After an hour we were able to slip away and backpedal through the brush, into the high country. By the end of the day we had just recovered the distance we traveled backwards. The light was gone and it was time for sleep.

We spent that first night near a mountaintop, sleeping in our parachutes. When we awoke in the morning, we discovered that we were within a few yards of a sheer cliff that dropped hundreds of feet to the forest floor below. We also found animal tracks all around us, including what we believed to be bear tracks.

The third night out it began to rain. It was October and it was cold. But in our parachute pack were slickers. Each slicker had snaps that allowed us to snap two slickers together providing us with a waterproof cover. I found a low-hanging branch and formed a lean-to shelter by placing the two slickers over the branch. We got into our sleeping bags under the slickers and went to sleep. An hour later I woke up sopping wet. I had made one small mistake. When I draped the slickers over the branch, I did so with the overlap facing up, not down. Instead of keeping the water off us, it funneled it right onto our sleeping bags.

I've never been so cold, wet, and miserable in my life.

By the fourth day I realized how stupid I had been to throw away the energy bars. Carlson offered me some of his. I deferred. I was hungry, but I was enthusiastic and thoroughly enjoying the trek. We made it to the end without getting caught. We had followed the advice of our instructor, we avoided the low country and the streams and the roads and took the toughest route imaginable, a route that an enemy would seldom take. It worked at Stead AFB and some months later it worked for a number of pilots who were shot down in North Korea.

The trucks picked us up and took us back to the base where a lavish turkey dinner with all the trimmings awaited. We were ravenous. We grabbed the tin-serving platter and crammed it full of food.

Unfortunately, about all we could get down was a mashed pea. In the past five days our stomachs had shrunk to the size of a walnut, and a small walnut at that.

Name, Rank, and Serial Number

The last night in Stead was by far the most memorable. All the crews gathered in a large semicircular outdoor stand and listened while the commandant of the base made an extraordinary speech. During WW II, he had been one of the top intelligence officers in the Air Force.

It was a cold October night and his presentation took more than an hour. Still there wasn't a rustle, a cough, or a fidget. He began by announcing that seventy percent of those who started the trek had been captured and his men got the classified information they sought from ninety percent of the captives.

"What does that tell you?" he asked. "It tells you that if you think you can get away with giving only your name, rank, and serial number, you are terribly mistaken. Remember, those of you who were captured knew that you would not be harmed. The Chinese and the North Koreans do not follow the rules of the Geneva Convention. We have proof of that. They will kill you if they see fit and your body will never be found. They are practicing a very new form of interrogation. It's called brainwashing and they are good at it. It's the kind of interrogation you want to avoid if at all possible. And the only way you can avoid it is if they think you are cooperating with them.

"So what do you do? You sing like a canary. You tell them anything they want to hear unless you know for a fact that it is top secret. Then you must be able to convince them that you don't know anything about that subject.

"The extraordinary thing is that if information was the only thing the Chinese and Koreans were seeking, there is enough latitude in the Convention rules to get all the information they wanted. Let me explain.

"In WW II, I followed the rules and still managed to break virtually every prisoner. Let me tell you a story about a beautiful young nymphet. Our intelligence group came across a picture of this young thing lying naked on a pool table somewhere in Paris. Behind the table, appreciating the sight, were a number of mid-to-high-ranking German officers. We called her Fifi and her picture made the rounds and then was filed. We throw nothing away in the intelligence service.

"We had been plagued by one particular German pilot in North Africa. He had shot down a number of American pilots and was deadly accurate. We wanted that man in the worst way and then one day we got him. He was shot down and I couldn't wait to interrogate him. He proved to be an Aryan son-of-a-bitch who rebuffed my attempts to get him to talk.

"'My name is Von Schultz, I am a colonel and my serial number is AO 2223846 and that is all I will tell you. You can kill me if you like.'

"We knew we could never break him and were about to send him on to his assigned POW camp when I sensed there was something familiar about the colonel. A day later it hit me. Fifi! My God, he was second from the end behind the pool table. The next morning I invited the colonel into my office. I told him that he would be posted that afternoon to a POW camp for officers and he seemed relieved. Then I mentioned, 'By the way, Colonel, did you know that your wife recently moved to Von Strasse Place in Berlin?'

"The colonel couldn't believe we knew about his wife's move. She had done so only the week before. 'We will send your wife a package through the Red Cross to let her know that you are safe. We would appreciate it if you would check the contents of the package before we post it.'

"I rang a buzzer and my sergeant entered carrying a manila envelope, which he handed the colonel. He opened it and pulled out the contents and as he did so, his face went stark white. The colonel retreated to the corner of the room, where he tore the picture of Fifi into a hundred shreds. Once again I rang the buzzer and the sergeant returned carrying fifty more envelopes, all properly stamped and addressed. 'When you finish destroying these, Colonel, we have a hundred more awaiting you.' He slumped down in the chair by my desk and said, 'What do you want to know?'

"We learned a great deal that day, all because we filed a picture of a nude girl."

The colonel lit a cigarette, drank from the glass by the podium then continued,

"We used the rules of the Geneva Convention to help us in our interrogation. For instance, the Geneva Convention stipulates that a prisoner may not be kept in solitary confinement for more than sixty days. We complied with this rule but we also found a way to stretch it. And, oh, how we stretched it!

"We had a German POW who was hard-core. We couldn't get any information from him, so we put him into a small holding cell with virtually no light. There was no room in which to exercise, nothing to read, no one to talk to, and no way to determine the passage of time, nothing but absolute boredom.

"At 8:00 in the morning, breakfast was shoved under the door. At 10:00 lunch followed. At 12:00 came dinner. The prisoner had three meals and so he assumed that was one day. At 3:00 in the afternoon breakfast came again and at 6:00 was lunch and so forth. Two days. At the end of five weeks, the prisoner, who had gained several pounds, screamed to his captors that it was inhuman to keep a man in solitary for three months. He agreed to tell all.

"Rules are rules and you can often make them work for you."

There were many other incredible stories told that night. There was one that topped all the rest, a story about a sergeant who successfully evaded interrogation.

"He did so by talking. When he was asked a question about his unit, the sergeant said, 'Oh, that's interesting, let me tell you about that. My dearest friend is in my unit. Would you believe I met him twenty years ago in kindergarten?' By the time the sergeant had graduated from kindergarten, three large books of shorthand had been filled. Every time they tried to redirect the sergeant, he found another path to follow. By the end of the week, even the Germans realized that they would get nothing of value from this soldier and he was posted to a permanent POW camp.

"Gentlemen, my advice to you," the colonel continued, "if you are captured, talk your head off. Forget that name, rank, and serial number shit. That exists only in Hollywood. You know what is top secret and what is not. Tell them whatever they want to know except what is top secret."

With that my two weeks at Stead AFB came to a close and I was on my way to Korea.

The P-47: An Anachronism

Marion Fisher prepares for his first flight in a P-47. Minutes later Marion would destroy this plane trying to land it with a runaway prop. Note the condition of the plane by the painted numbers.

While I was doing my best to avoid being caught at Stead, Marion Fisher, a member of 52-Charlie, was posted to a base in Kansas to check out in the T-33. The ink was hardly dry on those orders. however, before they were changed. Fisher was sent to Craig AFB in Alabama to check out in the P-51. Those orders didn't last long enough to be put in Marion's 201 file. Next he was told to report to the 105th Fighter Squadron in Knoxville, Tennessee. By the time he got to Knoxville the squadron designation was changed to the 469th.

Finally Fisher was on a base with an assignment. It was now September and he had been on the road in search of a home since he graduated in May. During that period he got little flying time, but he learned how to pack and unpack.

Fisher now had a BOQ, a mess hall, and a post-office address. All he needed was a plane to fly.

And there it was, waiting for him. The T-6.

Marion Fisher was certain he was going to be stuck with the T-6 for the duration. Eventually, however, a P-47 became available, the P-47 Thunderbolt—A WW II anachronism. The P-47 flying days had ended in 1945. More than fifteen thousand had been built and it was the dominant fighter in WW II. The P-47 had a Pratt and Whitney R-2800 radial engine the size of a small house. It was affectionately called the Jug. And it could fly for hours with one or two of its cylinders shot out.

God knows why anyone was checked out in the 47 eight years after the plane was designated for mothballs. Replacement parts were few and the plane was old and tired and had no military value in the jet age. Most had been flown to the bone yard in Tucson.

Fisher had his orders and now he had a plane, but how in God's name was he going to get checked out? There were no two-seater 47s. Most of his preflight training was spent in a simulator. However, the day arrived when he could no longer delay his solo. A chase pilot was assigned to fly his wing should he need help.

Fisher completed his walk-around, put on his chute, taxied to the runway, and began his takeoff. Just as he broke ground the reduction gear failed and he was nursing a runaway prop, one of the most dangerous situations a pilot can encounter. If your prop goes too fast, it becomes a wall and, instead of taking chunks out of the air, it adds so much drag the plane will not fly.

Fisher managed to climb to 500 feet by juggling the throttle to keep the prop under control. He throttled back to maintain a 140-knot speed and tried to call the chase plane, but his radio was dead. He looked around for a friendly pasture in which to land, but there were only hills, trees, and a railroad track. Marion's choices were limited. He was not high enough to bail out, so he'd have to try to return to the airport and, with a hand from the good Lord, land that Jug on a piece of cement. He selected runway number 22 right but overshot it and aimed for 22 left. It had been raining for ten days and mud was everywhere. Fisher missed both runways and set his crippled 47 down in a field of mud, roared across a couple of taxi strips, across another unnamed runway which thank God was not in use, through another patch of mud, and finally hopped up onto his chosen runway, 22R.

Fisher parked on the end of the runway and turned his switches off. He'd been in the air less than ten minutes. Fortunately, the Air Force retired the 47 shortly thereafter and as far as Fisher was concerned, not a moment too soon.

Marion not only missed the runway, he also missed flying in Korea, which he regrets. Nonetheless, flying was his chosen career. He flew for thirty-eight years, ending up as a United Airlines captain. In all those years he never had a more harrowing experience than the time he flew a P-47. Still, he considers himself fortunate. Henry Stephens, 52-Charlie, was killed in a P-47 accident in Fort Knox about the same time as Fisher was tearing up the mud fields in Knoxville.

Finally, after some harrowing experiences in a P-47, Marion Fisher gets to fly in a real plane.

The Christmas That Never Was

Goodbye Reno, goodbye Stead. It was time to go to war. On Christmas Eve 1952 I boarded a Military Air Transport Service plane bound for Hawaii along with a hundred or so other pilots, bombardiers, and navigators. I anticipated having a few rum drinks on the beaches of Oahu and going for a swim in its warm waters. That was not to be. The MATS plane landed at Hickam AFB, refueled, and immediately took off. A few hours later we landed at Johnson Island, a speck in the Pacific ocean, seven feet high at its highest point, composed of coral and bird droppings and so small that the runway started in the ocean, ran through the island and ended in the ocean.

We refueled, enjoyed a sandwich and a bottle of beer, and then continued our flight to Japan. A few hours later we crossed the international dateline and Christmas day disappeared in the throbbing of an engine. Our next stop was Wake Island where eleven years earlier the Japanese had overpowered the American garrison stationed there. The scars of that horrible battle were still visible, including a Japanese gun emplacement and a pillbox with its three-foot-thick cement walls horribly mangled by several hundred 50-caliber bullets. There were empty hard stands for the Japanese Zero and a landing craft with its bow sticking above the water, slowly rusting, slowly giving back the terrible memories of dying men. I tried to visualize what had taken place there and realized my final destination would be much like the lonely beaches of Wake Island, with its painful memories of death and sacrifice. When I re-boarded our MATS plane, I did so with a somber mindset. I was on my way to war, along with a hundred other young men my age, many of whom would be killed.

From top left: Beached troop carrier, a Japanese torpedo, mess kitchen, hard stand for planes. Pictures taken at Wake Island.

Part Two

The War in the Skies over Korea

Kadena Air Force Base, Okinawa

It had been only seven years since Okinawa ran red with the blood of Americans and Japanese, seven years since beached LSTs and partially sunken naval vessels and toppled tanks and shattered guns and broken aircraft and mangled bodies and blackened caves had littered the landscape.

Now Okinawa could easily have passed for a Caribbean paradise, with a golf course and civilian and military airfields and some of the most beautiful beaches in the world. The only constant reminder that this was not a vacation trip were the hard stands at Kadena, filled with B-29s whose bellies had been painted black so they could not be seen at night from the ground, a pair of antiaircraft guns guarding the base, and strings of brass 50-caliber machine gun cartridges that seemed to stretch forever placed meticulously beside each plane. Cradled beside the cartridge belts were 500-pound bombs, each with a yellow stripe painted on its nose.

Kadena AFB on Okinawa would be home for the next six months. I would fly twenty-seven combat missions from here to North Korea and back. Each mission would be at least eleven hours long, during which our 29 would drop more than one thousand five-hundred-pound bombs on enemy territory.

The day after we arrived, I was introduced to my new Airplane Commander…let's call him John Smith—and to my new crew. Capt. John Smith was a retread from WW II, with a distinguished combat record. Our radar operator, Lieutenant Sharp, proved to be the best in the squadron.

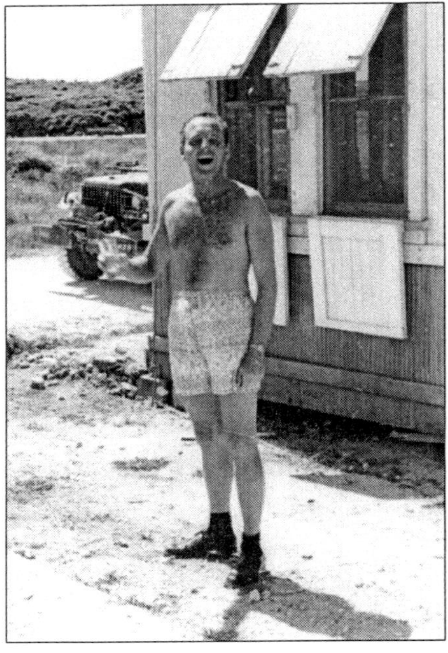

Captain Smith-AC Lieutenant Sharp-Radar, Capt. Dudendorf-Bombardier

Our bombardier, Captain Dudendorf, was a happy-go-lucky man with a perpetual smile—a joy to be around and a generous and outgoing individual. He too saw service in WW II. But now his only assignment was to supervise the loading and arming of the bombs and the opening of the bomb-bay doors

Our navigator, whose name I no longer recall, was a major and a funny little man. He was an excellent navigator. There would be no lost Mississippi River on his watch. In all the missions I flew I never gave a second thought to navigation.

The most important member of any crew was the flight engineer. And we had the very best, Staff Sergeant Mackenzie. He knew everything there was to know about the R-3350 engine. He could tell by listening whether the engine was operating efficiently and above all, he never panicked.

The planes flying in Korea were eight years old as were their engines. Virtually every pilot lost at least one engine from mechanical failure. It was the flight engineer's responsibility to assure that the engines ran smoothly. When an engine failed in flight, the engineer feathered the propeller by turning the blades into the wind, so that it would not create a drag and jeopardize the safety of the crew. A radio

Sergeant Mackenzie-Flt Engineer, Sergeant Boswick-Right Gunner

Corporal Moreland, Tail Gunner, Corporal Oku-Radio Operator

operator and four gunners filled out the crew. During the early stages of the Korean War B-29s were shot down on virtually every combat mission. They were no match for the MiG-15. In late December 1952, Far Eastern Air Force Operations canceled all further daylight-bombing missions. The B-29 would fly combat only under the cover of darkness. Fortunately, the MiG didn't have on-board radar, so they couldn't find the B-29 at night.

Private Railton-Central Fire Control Sergeant Auger-Left Gunner

The Moment of Truth

On January 8, 1953, I was scheduled to fly my first combat mission. My day began at the crack of dawn, twelve hours before takeoff. I met my crew at the hard stand where each member was given a specific assignment to prepare the plane for war. The gunners were responsible for loading the ammunition, the brass shells glowing red in the early morning sun. The silhouette of a gunner kneeling on top of the plane beside a gun turret was an Ansel Adams photograph, and the ninety-nine foot fuselage, with its blackened belly and its hand-rubbed stainless steel top, created a diamond-like setting for the glass-house cockpit twinkling in the reflections of a sun rising from a deep sleep. A small tractor towed a line of forty cradles filled with five-hundred-pound bombs and parked it in the hard stand next to the B-29. The engineer removed the cowling from an engine and pulled the prop through, then asked me to start the engines. When he was satisfied the engines were performing well, I shut them down. The cowlings were replaced, the sumps bled, tanks topped off, flaps raised and lowered, bomb bays checked, and the log signed. Then the bombardier supervised the loading of forty 500-pound bombs.

The 29 was now ready to deliver its payload of death.

The officers attended a briefing session, learned the name of the target and what interdiction could be anticipated. The IP (intercept point) and AP (aiming point) were defined. Tonight's mission was a milk run, a walk in the park. And we had a safety factor. A seasoned combat pilot would be riding with us as a check pilot—standard operating procedure for any crew flying their first combat mission.

The crew prepares. Check the chutes, the life vests, the flak jackets. Your life may depend on how well you check.

At dusk we stood by our 29 checking our chutes and preparing for the night ahead. Engines were started and fifteen fully loaded B-29s moved slowly toward the end of the runway. The tower flashed a green light. Captain Smith pushed the throttles forward and the lumbering giant began to move, slowly, inexorably down the ten thousand-foot runway carrying eleven airmen and a fully loaded bomb bay.

I called out the ground speed and when we reached 110 knots, Smith pulled back on the yoke and the B-29 eased off the runway just before it turned into the Pacific Ocean and gently lifted into the starless sky.

We'd been in the air only a short time when a warning siren blasted and red lights filled the cockpit. Fire flashed across the starboard wing then dimmed into trailing sparks that drew an endless dotted line across the night.

"Jesus Christ, what the hell was that?" I yelled.

"Pull the power off three!" the flight engineer screamed. "Now!"

I pulled the power off and the flight engineer hit the feather button, turning the propeller's leading edge into the wind-stream so the prop wouldn't windmill and create drag. Captain Smith did his best to hold the overloaded plane in the sky. The prop slowly came to rest and our 29 moved quietly through the night, unmindful of the drama just ended.

"Okay, Sergeant, what happened?"

"I have no idea, sir. Oil pressure was low, but not dangerously. We'll have to see when we open her up."

"Bombardier, prepare to dump our load," Captain Smith ordered. "We're going to abort."

"Forget that, Captain," Steve Walter, the check pilot, said calmly.

"Excuse me? What did you say?"

"We're not aborting this mission, Smith."

Captain Walter had spoken. Walter was a ruggedly handsome man, square-jawed, with hands that were carved for the yoke of a bomber. Confidence oozed from every pore of his body, and his eyes twinkled with determination and humor.

"Gentlemen, we've been given ten tons of bombs and a target. We are only a couple of hours away and we have three engines that will carry us safely there and back. We're not dropping these bombs in the ocean, so sit back and enjoy the flight."

"But, Captain, we can't make altitude," I said.

"Tell me something I don't know, Lieutenant. When we get to Korea we'll call ground control and they'll give us a front line target. We'll go in at the altitude they assign us."

"Roger, sir."

As Airplane Commander, it was Captain Smith's decision whether to abort or fly the mission. Walter and Smith were both captains, but Walter was light years Smith's superior and Smith was wise enough not to challenge him.

Smith called to the engineer, "Sergeant, clean up the aircraft, lean it out and watch the cylinder-head temperatures."

We had nine hours yet to fly and our safety factor was feathered. It was going to be a long night. Over the next four hours the three engines droned on somniferously. It was a beautiful night for flying.

No turbulence, no weather. The benign ocean spread out in front of us, a dark gray mantle, with crooked rivers of moonlight dancing toward the horizon.

Smith tapped the yoke and pointed to me. I took control and switched on the automatic pilot. The captain unclipped his oxygen mask, undid his throat mike, and stretched out in his seat. In the missions that followed, he always slept on the way to the target and I slept on the way back. There is something soporific about the drone of Allison engines in perfect sync. It was a lullaby sung by unseen sirens.

Soon the tip of South Korea was etched onto the radar screen. I switched off the automatic pilot and tapped Smith on the arm.

"Korea, sir."

"Roger, Gushee, it's mine. Call ground support and find out if they have a target."

I didn't like front-line bombing one bit. Some kid on the ground whom I had never met would assign us our altitude and our ground speed and tell us when to release our bombs. If he were accurate, the trench we hit would be the enemy's. If not … well, you don't like to think about that.

My earphones crackled. "Seven seventy-four, we can sure use you. You're ten minutes from the target. Take up a heading of 350 and drop down to four thousand feet."

"Roger."

"I'll take over at the IP, sir," the unseen voice from the ground said. "Please do exactly as I say. There are a lot of ass-busting mountains nearby and your bomb run will be below most of them."

"Thanks for that little bit of happiness. By the way, what's your rank?" I asked.

"Staff sergeant, sir."

"Great. I'm going to get my butt crushed by a goddamn NCO."

"No sir, you're not. I do this several times a night and I haven't lost one yet…now sir, you are approaching the target. Drop to 2800 feet and turn left three degrees to a heading of 347…please open your bomb bay doors now…thank you, sir. Once you have released your bombs, sir, climb to 5,000 feet and take up a heading of 175 degrees.

When you reach that altitude, you are on your own...thirty seconds to bombs away...don't touch the pickling button until I tell you. One second early and we hit our troops. Ten seconds to drop...count with me. Five...four...three...two...one...release!"

Smith pulled back on the yoke and the 29, now ten tons lighter, responded like a homesick angel. But as we leveled off at five thousand, our B-29 shivered. A ghostly feeling sent pins dancing up and down my spine.

The tail gunner called, "Captain, we got fire from number two and it's licking the elevators."

"Handle it, Gushee," Smith ordered.

"Roger. I'm pulling the power off two but let's not feather it just yet. Engineer, what's going on?"

"Looks like a turbo torch, sir."

"Navigator, give us a heading to the nearest base."

"Excuse me, Lieutenant, mind if I fly for a bit?" Captain Walter was standing behind me. I gave him my seat and watched as he took control from Smith without even asking. He guided the plane as gently as a sommelier poured a fine wine. "What's the heading, navigator?"

"187 degrees, sir. K-2 at Taegu."

"Turning to 187. Engineer, I agree with the lieutenant, let's leave it turning in case we need it for landing."

One feathered, one wind milling, and smoke trailing the aircraft. Prayers come easily at a time like that.

Fortunately, we were only minutes away from a base in Taegu. But it was night, and the field was barely visible.

"K-2 tower, this is 774 heavy with a couple of engines out. Can you give us a direct in approach?"

"Roger 774, you're cleared. Be advised we're in a bowl here, mountains on all sides. We can turn the runway lights on but for a few minutes only. We're expecting Bed-Check Charlie. You understand."

"Roger, tower, I'll have this bird on the runway in less than two minutes."

Captain Walter put the wing tip of our 29 in the center of the

Home of the F-84 fighter-bomber and of McDonnell, Fuller, Kelly, and a bunch of others from 52-Charlie.

runway and turned around it until we lost four thousand feet. Our downwind, our base, and our final were all in a forty-five degree turn. And when Walter landed our aircraft, he did so without the squeal of a tire or a telltale puff of smoke.

We taxied off the runway, shut down the engines, and exited the aircraft. Sergeant Mackenzie popped the Zeus fasteners, pulled the cowling off the sick engine and said quietly, "Come here, Lieutenant. You have to see this."

"My God, Sergeant, is that puddle in the power section what I think it is?"

"Yes, sir. High-octane gas! If the captain had added power during landing, we would be scattered from here to the front lines. There wouldn't be enough left of us to fill a dustpan. We're damn lucky it didn't blow."

"Something you can tell your grandchildren about, Lieutenant," a smiling Captain Walter said softly.

"Tell me, Captain, are all first missions like this?"

"No. Only a lucky few."

Someone touched my shoulder, "For Christ sake, it's the Mole! (my nickname from college). What are you doing in Taegu, slumming?"

It was the officer of the day, Quinn Fuller, a man I had not seen since we graduated from primary. He went to fighters while I went to multi-engine school.

Quinn Fuller before he learned what it was like to fly a Napalm run. He was smart enough to keep his chute within arm's reach.

Fuller was a cocky young man with an air of invincibility. He was one of the first to solo in a T-6 at Greenville. I told him about my night in the sky, expecting a degree of veneration. But Quinn shrugged his shoulders and stifled a yawn, a bit too blasé for my taste. I left Quinn at the flight line and went to the officers' club for a scotch and soda —where I met my old nemesis, "Your-gear-is-down!" Chappy McDonnell. We ordered a couple of drinks and I told Chappy about my first combat mission and he was impressed. I mentioned that I met Fuller on the flight line but he seemed bored when I told him my story.

"Ah," McDonnell chortled, "did Quinn tell you about his first combat mission?"

"No, he didn't say a word."

"Well, let me buy you another drink, we'll need the time."

The officers' club was filled with pilots who had flown two combat missions that day and watched as one of their comrades was blown to pieces. No one goes to bed in a war and you never forget names, but faces disappear quickly.

Two Hours to Hell and Back

"Three weeks ago Fuller flew his first combat mission," Chappy began. "His target was on the Haeju peninsula. Takeoff was normal. The flight there took only fifteen minutes. Mole, you know anything about the F-84?"

"No, can't say I do."

"It's a 'just-miss' aircraft. It hasn't the speed of an F-86 or the maneuverability of the 80. Still the Air Force bought a whole bunch of them and did the only thing they could. They turned them into tactical fighters and gave them to a group of know-nothing cadet graduates. Yeah, the 84 is a mother's worst dream. Still, it beats the piss out of a, excuse the expression, B-29."

I let that pass. After all, I was on his turf.

"Quinn was scheduled to make a napalm run. That's when you drag your tail through the treetops and drop your bomb and hope to hell you can climb above the explosion. If you like chicken, this is your game.

"Quinn began his run at forty feet…"

"Forty feet? Bullshit!"

"Oh, you were there, were you?"

"Okay, forty feet, if you say so! But that's not even a good-sized tree."

"You're right about that. Anyhow, Quinn released his napalm and watched the flame spread below him. He felt a bump and noticed that a few bullets had pierced his canopy and his right wing was on fire. Every warning light in the cockpit was on, including the fire-warning light.

"Quinn had been told that once your fire-warning light comes on, you have about seven seconds before your plane blows up. He was too low to bail out and he knew it would take longer than seven seconds to get to altitude. So he pulled back on the stick and you know what that cocky son-of-a-bitch said to himself while he was climbing?"

"I give up."

"Seven seconds? How do they know?"

"When Fuller reached 1100 feet, he was hit by ground fire once again and a wing blew off. It was time to get the hell out so Quinn blew the canopy and ejected."

"Holy shit, Quinn didn't say a word about it at the flight line."

"You know Quinn, he doesn't talk a lot about himself. Anyhow, he hurt his back and his leg bailing out. His chute opened and he had an amusement park ride to the ground. Or so he thought.

"The gooks had formed a circle below him and shot at him as he descended. He was hit in the forehead and blood began dripping through his eyes and down his face. It soaked his scarf and his Mae West.

"The members of his flight formed a cap and strafed the bastards, then called in F-80s and F-51s for further support.

"Quinn landed in a rice paddy, which was being tended by Korean farmers. He was completely exposed so he took off for the tall grass still wearing his chute. He forgot about the quick-release snaps so he started cutting the risers with a knife.

"Two enemy soldiers came running towards Quinn firing their rifles. Bullets sped over his shoulders and past his head. Quinn fell forward to avoid the rifle fire and splashed into a rice paddy, and you know what they use to fertilize rice paddies?"

"I do, not a good fall."

"While he was in the paddy, he pulled out his .45, aimed at the soldiers who were chasing him and pulled the trigger, but because he was so scared he forgot to inject a cartridge into the chamber.

"George Clapman, a member of 52-Baker, who according to Quinn was the worst shot in gunnery school, caught one of the Koreans in his sights and fired a short burst.

"The man absolutely disintegrated. The other soldier decided he'd had enough of war and raced toward the protective reeds on the other side of Fuller. He realized he could make it faster if he tossed away his rifle, which he did.

"He damn near stepped on Quinn on his way to the reeds. Quinn changed directions slightly so they wouldn't be sharing the same reeds and continued to fire his .45 as he ran, or at least he thought he was firing his .45.

"Both men reached the tall grass," Chappy continued. "Both hid from each other. Quinn threw away his Mae West and yellow scarf to better blend into the reeds. Both were soaked with blood. Quinn watched as the 84s, 80s, and 51s kept making passes, firing at anything that moved. This went on for about an hour until the cap began to run low on fuel. The 84s had to return to base but the others did their best to keep the enemy pinned down until a chopper could pick Fuller up.

"Fuller's URC-4 radio crackled. Owen Clark, a helicopter pilot, reported to Quinn he was on the way. An eternal few minutes later, the copter arrived and dropped a sling. Quinn slipped into the sling, and the 'copter took off with Quinn dangling at the end of a very long rope with no parachute. The F-80s and the P-51s retired. The gooks stood up and started shooting at Quinn again as he swung back and forth a few hundred feet above them. A winch pulled Quinn toward the cockpit.

"You should ask Quinn to describe the sound bullets make when they pass within an inch of your ears. He can do it, I can't."

I finished my third scotch and ordered a fourth. I had too much whiskey and too little sleep, still I saw everything that Chappy said.

"Finally, Quinn reached the 'copter. He was frightened and failed to follow the instructions. Instead of holding the rope, he reached up and grabbed the floor of the helicopter...and slipped out of the sling..."

"Oh, bullshit, Chappy, this sounds like the Perils of Pauline."

"Believe it or not, that's what happened. Elmer Davis, a medic inside the 'copter held on to Fuller's jacket despite the fact his hands were freezing. He screamed at Clark to land because he couldn't hold Fuller much longer. Clark landed under heavy fire, and Davis pulled Fuller into the chopper.

"Okay, how did it end?"

"Owen flew back to K-16 where the medics bandaged Quinn's wounds. He had lost a lot of blood and his blood pressure was dangerously low. So the doctors prescribed eight ounces of whiskey. Quinn swears that all Air Force doctors are alcoholics. Before the night was finished, Fuller was flown to a second base where he again received the prescribed eight ounces of whiskey and then finally returned to K-2.

"True?"

"True!"

"Well, maybe that explains the yawn!"

"Yeah, maybe."

They say that everything is relative. I agree. Two blown engines aren't worth the scotch it takes to forget them. I will never think of Korea again without seeing a man dangling at the end of a long rope as bullets speak to him in their own special tongue.

Quinn Fuller was awarded the Distinguished Flying Cross, the Bronze Star, and the Purple Heart. Owen Clark, who had volunteered for this mission after the 'copter that was assigned to pick up Fuller had a suspiciously "rough engine," was also awarded the DFC. Elmer Davis, the man who held onto Fuller's flight jacket and who had also volunteered for this hazardous mission, received only a thank you from Fuller, nothing from the Air Force.

Quinn Fuller and Owen Clark continued to petition their congressmen year after year to have Elmer Davis recognized for his bravery. After fifty-plus years this oversight was corrected. On February 11, 2005, fifty-two years after the incident, a four-star general, John Handy, presented Elmer Davis with the Distinguished Flying Cross in a special Air Force ceremony attended by Quinn Fuller and Owen Clark.

Happy-go-lucky Quinn Fuller prepares to take off on his first combat mission in a borrowed F-84. Notice the napalm bomb below the wing in the top picture. About an hour later, his wing blew off and he bailed out. When asked what he had done to the plane he responded, "I broke it."

Taegu...A War-Ravaged City

My sleep was interrupted early the next morning by the sound of jet engines. I looked out of my BOQ and watched a flight of F-84s take off and head north. Each plane carried bombs under its belly and was loaded with 50-caliber ammunition. There would be a few North Koreans who would miss supper that night and all the nights to follow.

I would like to have flown with them on a mission. There is an excitement about single-engine planes that we bus drivers missed. Our missions were eleven hours long. Theirs were an hour. They could leave their drink in the officers' club and be back before the ice melted. In the time it took to load a 29, the jet jockeys could fly two missions. But there were compensations. A fighter pilot's combat tour was 100 missions. A B-29 pilot had to fly only twenty-five to thirty. Just as important, if you lose an engine in a bomber, you simply pull off the power, tell the engineer to feather the prop, trim the aircraft, and resume listening to Armed Forces radio. If you lose an engine in a fighter, you pop the canopy and bail out.

I was in no hurry that morning. I had nowhere to go and nothing to do. There were no B-29 engines on the base. They had to be brought in from Tokyo along with a crew to mount them. We would remain at K-2 for a week before our 29 would be ready to take us back to our base in Okinawa. K-2 was about as exciting as the bottom of a birdcage. The base boasted a decent mess, an officers' club with the cheapest drinks in the hemisphere, Bed-Check Charlie, and a nurse in her fifties. That week would change my life. Steve Walter, the man I was trying desperately to hate, would become my bridge partner, one

Captain Steve Walter. Exceptional pilot, extraordinary man.

of my dearest friends, and ultimately an usher at my wedding. Steve Walter was the finest pilot and the most dedicated officer I ever met.

One afternoon Steve and I decided to visit Taegu, the South Korean city bordering K-2. It was about a hundred miles from the front lines, but the turmoil of war was present on its streets and in the faces of its citizens. Shacks littered the main street, most of which had suffered war damage either when the UN drove north or the Chinese drove south. Taegu was an unclaimed town with alliances that changed every time a new army marched through. Bomb craters decorated streets that were filled with stink and offal. Merchants reached out from foul-smelling shops and offered their wares at give-away prices. Nuts roasting on charcoal fires were sold on every corner. Little boys and little girls all had something they were told they must sell to the "GIs."

The town was a bustle of activity. The dispossessed, in varying degrees of filth and squalor, streamed through the main street, heading south. Their homes, those who had them, were in disputed territory. Their possessions were no longer theirs and their next meal was often found floating in the gutter or at the bottom of a garbage bin. Their eyes were opaque, their cheeks gaunt, any semblance of hope had long since faded.

All except the children who invented ways to amuse themselves. Attitudes were bright and smiles were broad. That day I saw the ravages of war in a very personal sense. It began when I noticed an older man whose legs had been blown off push himself along the street on a makeshift skateboard with padded hands. His clothes were tattered and his face sallow, and he wore a shiny steel helmet.

"Why, Steve? Why the helmet?" I asked.

The answer came quickly. A group of waggish kids ran at the cripple and beat him on the head with the sticks they carried solely for that purpose. It was a game, the only game in town. And the kids loved it.

No sooner had the old man disappeared down the street than a ten-year-old urchin tugged at my sleeve and said brightly, "Hey, GI, you want my sister? She's twelve, fucks good. You like her. Come on, five dollars, all day."

I had seen enough of war and I'd never heard a shot fired.

"Let's go back to the base, Steve. I haven't the stomach to stay longer."

"Yeah, let's."

Just then, an eight-year-old boy started across the street and was hit by a middle-aged Korean riding a bicycle. The man was thrown to the pavement but was unhurt. The boy lay semi-conscious in the street, bleeding from wounds to his head and body. The man got back on his bike and threatened the lad in a language I didn't understand. He kicked the boy in the stomach, spat on him, and then rode off. The boy remained bleeding in the street.

Fortunately there was an American MP nearby who took the lad to the base hospital.

Soldiers fight and die in battlefields, often under the most heinous conditions. But even in the mud and filth of a battle, nothing compares to the suffering of those who are innocent bystanders.

Steve was a religious man. Still he could not explain why God had forsaken this small part of hell. It would be months before I attended church again.

When I returned to the base, I went directly to the officers' club where I met Quinn Fuller who offered to buy me a drink. I asked him about his first combat mission. Quinn showed me a small scar on his forehead and smiled, "It was different, Mole. Don't think I want to do it again, but you know the interesting part? From the time I took off until the time I got back, just over two hours had passed."

"Two hours? You're kidding!"

"No, it's all there in the log. But enough about missions, how would you like to go up in a T-33?"

"I'd love it. When?"

"Tomorrow, I'll file a flight plan and check out a suit and mask for you."

"Great!" I knew from Quinn's smile that he fully intended to get me sick the next day. After all that's SOP (Standard Operating Procedure) for a jet jockey when he gets a trash hauler in his bird. We closed the bar that night and I turned in, looking forward to the adventure I knew I would have the next day.

God Must Be a Single-Engine Jockey

"Move your ass, Gushee. We have some flying to do!"

"Goddamn it, Fuller, don't you stove-pipes ever sleep! I'm on vacation here."

"Bullshit, Mole. This is no R & R. And you'll find that out when I get you upstairs. See you at the flight line in an hour."

"Roger, asshole. I'll be there."

The friends you make in the service are friends forever. You trust them, you respect them, you'd do anything for them, including sacrificing your life if need be. No one has an agenda. There are no heroes in a BOQ and there is no pomposity at twenty thousand feet or conceit in the mess hall. There is no avarice in the gaming rooms, or egotism in debriefing. That's the beauty of the service.

I met Fuller at flight-line supply where I checked out a suit, oxygen mask, helmet, and parachute. Bomber pilots and single-engine jocks don't even dress the same.

"Follow me, Mole," Fuller ordered.

We walked to a hard stand, where a bright T-33 stood waiting. The T-33 is a jet trainer with a tandem seat for the student pilot. It's a beautiful aircraft with intake manifolds molded into its side and a tricycle landing gear smaller than that of a children's bike. It has straight wings and a greenhouse canopy that stretches toward the exhaust manifold. Sitting there in the morning sun, the T-33 was a work of art, beautiful, gentle, and deadly.

"Need a leg up, Mole?"

"No, I think I can manage."

We climbed into the aircraft and Fuller lit the fuse. The T-33 now took on a very different personality. It was in charge, no longer a gentle piece of art. It was now a free-range mustang, convinced it could never be ridden.

Fuller taxied the plane to the end of the runway. There was an unusual sound in the cockpit, a gushing sound.

"What the hell's that noise? Is that you, Mole?"

"You're damn right it is, Fuller. I've got it on one-hundred-percent oxygen and that's where it's going to stay. You're not going to get me sick today!"

Fuller smiled to himself and shoved the throttle forward. The small jet responded with enthusiasm. As we roared down the runway, Fuller announced, "Mole, notice the mountain at the end of the runway. It's called 'bust-your-ass-hill.' It's an 84 graveyard."

Strewn across the rising slope of bust-your-ass-hill was a mangled F-84.

I remembered the day I soloed and my feeling of exhilaration. That feeling returned as we took over the sky that morning. It's the feeling the whole world is yours and you can do anything with it you want. You are a kite without a string and you can move in any direction you wish with the slightest movement of a stick.

"Okay, Mole. We're at ten thousand and the plane is yours. Can you give me a couple of rolls without losing a thousand feet?"

"You're damn right I can." I proceeded to show Fuller how wrong I was as I did two aileron rolls and lost several hundred feet.

"You sure have forgotten a lot since I last saw you. A hint. Keep the nose above the horizon and forget the stick, use the trim tab. This isn't a 29, it's very sensitive."

My next rolls were semi-perfect, and then I was at Greenville again, tearing holes in the sky, doing every imaginable maneuver and enjoying myself immensely.

"I got it, Mole. Let me show you how we go to war. First a dive-bombing run. I'll take it up to thirty thousand. See that small farmhouse below us? That's our target."

We were at thirty thousand before I could take a breath. Fuller flipped the plane on its back and aimed the craft at the farmhouse far below us. When we reached five thousand feet, he pulled back the stick.

"Bombs away. Goodbye, farmer."

The plane righted itself and within a short breath we were flying straight and level.

"Still got your breakfast?"

"You bet your sweet ass I have."

"Next, the napalm run. Here we go in at about fifty feet, drop our napalm and pull up as fast as we can. There's a small bridge a couple of miles from here, which will be our target today. Sit back and enjoy."

Fuller put the 33 on the tops of the trees and I swear I could count the birds nesting there. Suddenly up ahead was a small footbridge and we were closing on it at an alarming rate. There was not sufficient room to fly under that damned bridge, but I didn't think we had the altitude to fly over it.

"Bombs away!"

We missed the bridge, thank God, leaving my stomach lying on top of it as we pulled into a vertical climb. The altimeter went wild and when we reached twenty thousand feet, Fuller executed a perfect Immelman.

"Mole, I think it's home-go time. You want to try and land this thing?"

"You'd let me land this thing? A bomber pilot with exactly one hour in a T-33? I must admit you're a hell of a lot braver than I am, but I'd love to take a shot at it."

"Not to worry, Mole. Five feet off the flight path and I'll take over. Just remember, the 33 is very sensitive. It's easier to land than the T-6 as long as you don't over-control. I'll handle the checklist, you got the plane."

I'm not sure whether I was more nervous soloing in the T-6 or landing that jet that morning. It turned out to be far easier than I had imagined.

"Not exactly a grease job, but not bad for your first effort."

Fuller took over and taxied the jet back to its hard stand and then yelled over his shoulder, "On to the officers' club, Mole, and the drinks are on you."

The T-33 is a wonderful plane to fly. Responsive, quick, enjoyable even at 20 feet above the deck.

I was delighted to buy. This was the only jet I flew during my five years in the Air Force and it was one of my most enjoyable experiences.

Later that afternoon, I met with our flight engineer. Two new engines had been mounted on our 29 and we had to check-fly the aircraft before leaving K-2 and returning to Okinawa. We couldn't find Smith, so Captain Walter and I took it up with the flight engineer and a member of the ground crew. We flew around the field a few times, shot a few touch-and-gos before returning to the hard stand. The plane checked out beautifully. Our R & R was over. It was time to return to Okinawa and re-enter the war.

Five hours later we touched down at Kadena. My first combat mission had taken just under a week to complete, while Lieutenant Fuller's first mission took just under two hours.

Flying Blind

Tom Tudor's picture goes here, or should. But during one of his moves, all his military memorabilia was lost, pictures, medals, everything. So just imagine a good-looking, fierce fighting machine and you have Tom.

Tom Tudor had his Mississippi River while training in the T-6 and created an international incident at the same time. Tudor and twenty-nine other student pilots were flying from Williams AFB in Phoenix to Long Beach, California. No one in his flight had an instrument card, so they were under orders to return to Phoenix if they encountered clouds along the way, which they did. They diverted back to Williams, as ordered, only to find the weather in Phoenix was no better. The flight of T-6s therefore headed back to Southern California, where it was reported the cloud cover was breaking up. By now, however, the thirty T-6s were running low on fuel.

Fortunately, they found a small hole in the clouds over California and every single T-6 dove through that hole like a bee in search of a hive. Tudor had grown up in the West and was familiar with the topography. He spotted the Salton Sea and knew that El Centro Naval Air Station was nearby so he guided the flight of concerned cadets to the navy field, where they landed safely.

Tudor was now officially in charge. What to do during the evening? He suggested they all go to the San Diego Bar near Mexicali, on the other side of the border. There they met a cowboy from Texas with yellow boots and a Stetson hat, for which Tom swapped his flying boots and various other military paraphernalia.

Picture it: An aviation cadet in yellow boots, cowboy hat, and flying suit.

Soon, as sometimes happens in a Mexican bar, a fight broke out and the thirty students scattered to the winds. Tom in his new yellow boots couldn't scatter quite as quickly as the others and was caught. A five-dollar bribe to a Mexican policeman got him through a small hole in the border fence and he made his way back to the base. How he got past the Shore Patrol dressed in yellow boots and a cowboy hat heaven only knows.

The aftermath was not pretty. It became an international incident and the cadets were reprimanded by many and often.

Tudor finished his training in the F-84 at Luke AFB in Phoenix before being sent to K-2 to fly combat. After his third mission, he was promoted to flight leader.

One night his flight was put on alert.

"What the hell is this alert stuff?" he asked his commanding officer.

"Nothing to worry about, just go sit in your planes until they call off the alert."

That was fine—until OPS scrambled the unit. They took off not knowing where they were going or what they were supposed to do. Once airborne, the tower directed them to "Kitty-able."

"Tower, what the hell is 'Kitty-able'?"

"Haven't you been briefed?" someone answered in disbelief.

"Not a word! But if you give me the co-ordinates, I'll find it somehow."

Find it they did. They dropped their bombs and returned.

Tudor flew thirty-two combat missions and only on a couple was he hit by ground fire. His crew chief always patched up his 84 quickly and had it ready for the next mission. There were times when Tudor wished his crew chief wasn't so damn efficient. He could have used a few days off.

Then one day Tudor returned from a napalm mission with green tree stains on the undersurface of his aircraft. A napalm run was normally flown on the deck, but Tudor overdid it a bit that day. There'd be hell to pay if his CO saw the stains, but his crew chief had them removed before the CO reached the flight line.

On his thirty-third combat mission, Tudor was not quite so fortunate. He was carrying two one-thousand-pound bombs, which he had just dropped on some bridges when his canopy was shattered and he felt a terrible burning sensation spread across his face, while blood dripped into his oxygen mask. His plane vibrated so badly Tudor thought he might have to bail out. After a moment of reflection, he decided to stay with the plane as long as possible. He climbed to 6000 feet and reduced power, which eliminated the vibration.

Tudor's wounds were serious. His left eye was blinded and he could see only about fifteen degrees to the right with his other eye. He ducked low into the cockpit to make out his compass reading. In a situation like this, you trust your instruments and not your gut. One other pilot Tudor knew had failed to follow his compass when he was hit and headed north instead of south. He was never heard from again. Tudor squinted at the compass and took up a heading south. He held his right eye open with one hand and guided the plane with his other. His flight leader, Jim LaRue, pulled alongside. Both planes switched to emergency frequency and LaRue assessed the situation. He told Tudor not to worry, that he would fly his wing and talk him back to South Korea. The first base they came to was K-13, which had a short runway. But it was a runway. Tudor made three passes at the field, but he could see only a blur. He was concerned about stalling, so he didn't pull off enough power even though LaRue kept telling him to do so. On his fourth pass, Tudor, now legally blind, told LaRue he had a feeling he was too hot to land and was going to take it around.

LaRue assured Tudor his speed was fine, that he was six feet over the runway, in perfect shape to land.

"Cut your power, Tom, level it off gently, that's it, looks great! When you touch down, raise the gear and let the plane come to a stop. The fire trucks are in position and will follow you down the runway. I'm sure there's a medic standing by to get you out of the aircraft."

Tudor swallowed hard and did as he was told.

As soon as he touched down, he shut off the electrical systems to avoid fire and then overrode the gear safety switch and raised the gear. His plane screeched to a stop on the runway. He unfastened his shoulder harness and started to open the canopy.

Now his problems really began. The canopy was stuck. He pushed his feet against the crash panel and tugged at the canopy handles, but the canopy would not budge. He smelled fire, but he couldn't see a thing.

Tudor doubled his efforts to release the canopy, when suddenly in one awful moment the canopy blew and he was ejected, seat and all. Witnesses claimed that Tudor soared forty to sixty feet in the air before landing on his shoulder.

He broke his clavicle but sustained no spinal injuries. The medics gave him a shot and he was whisked off to Johnson AFB in Tokyo where he spent the next seven months going through one eye surgery after another. The sight in his left eye never improved, but he did get the vision back in his right eye.

Most pilots, at this stage in their career, would turn in their wings, get as large a disability as possible, retire to a comfortable civilian job, and begin to enjoy the rest of their lives.

Not Tudor. He wanted to stay in the service and fly, but there aren't a lot of one-eyed pilots in the USAF and he knew that, so he memorized the eye charts and every time he was given an eye test, he passed. The doctors realized what he was doing so they changed the charts as often as they could. But one glance with the good eye and Tudor had the chart memorized. The one man he couldn't fool was his commanding officer, who told Tudor he would rather fly with him than with virtually any other pilot on the base.

Tudor was given a waiver by his commanding officer and stayed in the service for the next three years, flying as a gunnery instructor pilot at Luke AFB.

A one-eyed gunnery instructor. Imagine that!

When Tudor left the service, he became a teacher and a farmer. Some might think he got a bad break. Not Tom Tudor. He treasures the time he spent in the Air Force and his memories of those years are among his fondest.

Joe Ortega and Jake the Lake Reider in Korea

I had the good fortune to talk to Joe Ortega and Jake Reider about their combat tours and they were kind enough to share their experiences with me.

Joe Ortega is as forthright as any man I've ever met. He began our conversation as follows, "Ted, if you don't mind, I am going to tell you a little bit about me before I tell you about my experiences."

"Sounds fine to me, Joe. You got the mike."

I wasn't sure what he was going to say, but I didn't expect what followed.

"Ted, I grew up an orphan in the slums of Kansas City. From the time I was seven until I was ten, I lived in the streets pushing drugs, stealing, pimping, and rolling drunks. I was a miserable punk. That's when Boys Town and Father Flanagan came calling. They took me in and changed my life forever. I have never forgotten them, nor will I ever. I even named my F-51 in Korea *Spirit of Boys Town.*

"I enlisted in 52-Charlie and after graduation from cadets, I was sent to Luke AFB in Phoenix to check out in the F-51 and then on to K-47 in Chinchong."

"How'd you like the 51?" I asked.

"Loved it. Greatest fighter ever made. It served me well. It kept me in the sky when a lot of other planes might not have."

"Tell me about some of your missions."

"Okay. When I arrived in Korea I was told that my first four com-

Joe Ortega and his F-51, Spirit of Boys Town.

bat missions would be milk runs. Indoctrination stuff, you know. No enemy action.

"Well, they lied!

"On my fourth combat mission, all hell broke loose. I was flying a bombing run with three other 51 pilots. The leader dove to the target and released his bombs, but he was hit. Number two and number three followed and they were also hit. Now it was my turn. Remember, Ted, this was supposed to be a milk run. I dove on the target, dropped my five-hundred-pound bombs, and returned to altitude. I was the only pilot in our group to make it back to K-47. The other three were forced to make emergency landings at other bases."

"That's a hell of a way to begin a combat tour. Your flight of four lost three aircraft. There had to be better days ahead."

"There were, and there weren't. A couple of weeks later while flying a napalm run my canopy was shot away and my helmet blew off. I ducked my head into the cockpit to keep it out of the slipstream. It was about twenty degrees below zero and the tears in my eyes were freezing. I made it back to my base, but my eyes were swollen shut and my face was black and blue from the top of my head to my throat. I could barely see the ground as I landed."

"Anything else?"

"Oh, sure! On another napalm run I was hit in the cooling coils, and you know about that?"

"Indeed I do, Joe, that's the most vulnerable part of the Mustang. Without cooling fluid, your engine will seize."

"You got it. I pulled my plane up sharply as I had to get altitude before the engine shut down. I set a course for Kimpo and declared a Mayday. The tower cleared me to land, but as I turned onto final, the tower reported that a C-47 on downwind was in trouble and ordered me to take it around. I told the tower, bullshit, I was going to land.

"They didn't take kindly to that. When my plane came to a stop on the runway, the officer of the day drove up, screaming every four-letter word he knew."

"What about the Gooney Bird (C-47)? Did it make it down okay?"

"Hell, yes, you flew the 47. That son-of-a-bitch can land on a bottle top. They put it down on the grass next to the runway, but there were several unhappy 86 pilots who were waiting to take off and couldn't because my plane was in the middle of the runway. We pushed it to the side and these jet jockeys came screaming down the runway flashing me the one-finger salute as they passed.

"I was pissed. The tower yelled at me. The OD yelled at me, The 86 pilots gave me the finger. So I yelled back at the OD. 'Goddamn, I called a Mayday. The tower accepted it. I had the right of way and I intend to write you bastards up, all of you bastards!'

"Cooler heads prevailed. They towed my 51 to a hangar, where the chagrined officer of the day apologized."

"Take a look at this," he said. The Mustang engine had melted. Had Ortega tried to take his plane around, he would have crashed.

Following his experiences in Korea, Joe Ortega flew combat in Vietnam and then spent most of his remaining years in the Air Force as an instructor pilot.

Ortega's admiration for Boys Town and Father Flanagan never flagged. Today, fifty-four years later, the initials of Boys Town are part of his e-mail address. If you ever have the opportunity to meet Joe Ortega, do so. He will tell you, as he has told me, that he credits Father Flanagan and Boys Town for redirecting his life. He said, "Many years ago Boys Town saved my life. There I learned the importance of God, family, and country. I volunteered for both Korea and Vietnam as a way of paying back my debt to Father Flanagan and to Boys Town."

Quite a man. Quite a pilot.

Jake Reider also had his moments in Korea.

"I flew 100 combat missions in Korea as a T-6 spotter pilot directing F-80s and 84s to ground targets. 99 of those missions were great. But, oh, that 100th mission!"

"Tell me about it, Jake."

"It started out like any other mission. No problem on the way to the target, but when I started my run I got caught in an ack-ack field. Shells burst all around my T-6. Suddenly oil spilled over my canopy, and I realized my engine would soon seize. I couldn't make it back to K-47. The only field within reach was K-18, which was a Republic of Korea air base. Do you know anything about K-18?"

"Not a thing."

"Well, it wouldn't have been my choice if I had one because it had a short runway with sand dunes all over the damn place. I was not looking forward to dead-sticking a T-6 into an unfamiliar base. God was with me that day, however. I landed without any problem, but my plane was so badly damaged I couldn't control it on the run out and hit one of those sand dunes with my wing tip, rupturing a fuel cell. My T-6 caught fire and burned out of control."

"Apparently you got out okay."

" I did and so did my observer."

Ortega and Reider had their moments in training and in combat and despite the fact that they both got lost as cadets; they found their way back to the States after their tour, without any problem whatsoever.

Old Four Eyes...The Man Who Relished Getting Shot At

Bill Vogel and his B-26 crew. Everyone else is looking at the camera. Vogel must be looking for his glasses.

Pilots are required to have 20/20 vision, but Bill Vogel was an anomaly. He wore glasses. He learned his vision was impaired when he tried to land the B-25 with its tricycle landing gear. He kept dropping it in from excessive heights. Command at Reese AFB was about to wash him out, when his instructor pilot petitioned both the Surgeon General and the Commanding General of the Air Training Command to give Vogel a dispensation. If either of these men had denied the petition, Vogel's flying career would have come to an end. But they didn't and Vogel became the only pilot ever to graduate from cadets who wore glasses. His fellow cadets kidded the life out of him. Their observation was, "How the hell did I get lucky enough to fly with old Four Eyes?"

Most people will do everything in their power to avoid being shot at, but not Vogel; he volunteered to be shot at while he was in Korea. He checked out in the B-26, a twin-engine tactical bomber, affectionately called the Widow Maker because so many pilots crashed during takeoff. But once mastered, it was a remarkable plane.

The war was winding down. Peace talks had begun in Panmunjom and fewer and fewer missions were being flown. Still, we were on a war footing and our antiaircraft gunners on the ground had to have something to shoot at. Bill Vogel volunteered to tow a target for gunnery practice. The tow cable was a mile long, which seemed to be plenty of margin for error. However, there were occasions when the radar-controlled guns on the ground locked on to the tow cable rather than the target and would walk up that cable toward the plane. If the radar was not shut off, it was goodbye B-26.

When he wasn't towing cable, Vogel was given other odd missions. One was to fly to the Yalu River to drop chaff in order to test the reaction of Chinese radar. He was flying a reciprocal engine aircraft in enemy territory, begging to be shot down by an enemy jet fighter. Fortunately, the Chinese did not scramble their MiGs.

Bill Vogel was used to danger. He seemed to thrive on it. During WW II as a seventeen-year-old, Vogel attended the merchant marine academy in New York. At that time, each cadet was expected to serve in a combat zone during the study program.

Bill was assigned to the *SS Wesleyan Victory*, a brand-new ship on its first voyage. There were three similar ships in his group. They were all carrying much-needed mortar ammunition for the invasion of Okinawa.

On May 27, 1945, Vogel was acting as the port loader on an antiaircraft gun when his ship was targeted by kamikazes. Three of the four new Victory ships carrying ammunition, *Hobbs, Logan,* and *Canada* were hit and blew up. A kamikaze missed the *Wesleyan* and hit the destroyer *DD Braine*, which was on the *Wesleyan*'s port side, killing sixty-six sailors. Bill Vogel and danger were constant companions.

Max Hanson, another future 52-C cadet, was also serving on a ship during the invasion of Okinawa, the *USS Converse*. Hanson watched as a torpedo hit the side of his ship fifteen feet below where he stood. It was a dud. Bill Vogel and Max Hanson made the same decision in the seas off Okinawa. They decided that if they ever had to go to war again, it would be in the air.

The Wesleyan *was the only Victory ship not sunk by a Kamikaze during the Okinawa campaign.*

Bill Vogel spent thirty years in the Air Force Reserve before retiring as a full colonel. Old Four Eyes is as active today as he was when he saw the world from the deck of a ship under attack by kamikazes, or from ten thousand feet being shot at by his own people, or from thirty thousand feet while tempting the Chinese Air Force to come shoot him down.

Someone asked Vogel to fly low so he could get a picture of his plane. Bill was quick to accommodate. Even the ants had to crawl back in their holes.

The Pilot Who Should Have Trained in Gliders

Harold Chitwood spent four-and-a-half years in the Air Force doing his very best to keep from becoming a statistic. On reflection, the odds were against him, but that never seemed to bother Chitwood. He had his Mississippi River, too. He had just completed his first solo night cross-country and was about to enter the pattern when his cockpit lights dimmed. Chitwood assumed his battery was failing. As he continued his approach all the lights in the plane, including his wing lights and landing lights, went out and, to make matters worse, he smelled smoke.

Chitwood's T-6 was on fire, and he had no radio, no way to contact the tower for landing instructions. He continued his approach, but when the tower saw an unidentified aircraft turning on to final it fired a red flare, ordering the pilot to abort his landing and leave the pattern. Chitwood was not about to comply. Instead he set his T-6 down, brought it to a stop, and climbed out as quickly as he could. The officer of the day, a major, chased the plane down the runway on a scooter, intending to ream the pilot out for not acknowledging the flare. But then he noticed the T-6 was on fire. He broke off and went to get help as quickly as his scooter could carry him.

After Chitwood graduated from cadets, he was assigned to an F-86 squadron in Korea where he had the pleasure of flying combat with Joe McConnell, America's leading ace in Korea. The pleasure came to an abrupt end one sunny afternoon. McConnell was flying flight leader with Chitwood as the element leader in # 3 position. In this formation, the flight leader and the element leader are the attack planes, with numbers two and four defending. They bumped into a flight of MiGs and McConnell immediately began to attack, with Chitwood on his wing. McConnell fatally wounded one of the MiGs and was making a second pass when his # 2 told him to break off, that a MiG was on his tail. McConnell, however, assumed that his wingman was overreacting and didn't heed the warning. But # 2 wasn't overreacting; there was a MiG on McConnell's tail, piloted by the Russian ace Semen Alexeivich Fedorets. Fedorets fired and hit McConnell who, in an extraordinary feat of flying, repositioned his critically wounded aircraft on Fedorets' tail and shot him down.

Joe McConnell, America's leading ace in Korea on the way to the Yalu with his flight, including Harold Chitwood in 881. Precise formation flying.

Chitwood took command and called Chodo Island requesting a rescue helicopter stand by. He and the other two members of the flight escorted McConnell to the Yellow Sea flying at eighty-five-percent power, just fast enough to maintain altitude and keep from stalling. #2 screamed once more, "Flight of MiGs at 6:00 o'clock high!" The MiGs had seen the smoke from McConnell's aircraft and apparently decided to finish him off. Chitwood and his two flying partners poured the coal to their planes and prepared to attack the MiGs but they beat a hasty retreat to the north. Chitwood returned to McConnell and finished escorting him to the coast, where a helicopter was waiting. McConnell bailed out and was in the water less than a minute.

The American Ace Joe McConnell at the Nest of the Cobras in Korea.

Chitwood was never credited with a kill, but he was credited with damaging three MiGs during three different missions, sending them back to Antung with their tails between their legs.

There were days when things didn't go quite as planned. On one of his missions, Chitwood's F-86 engine quit over the Yalu River. What followed was a silence a pilot never wants to hear over enemy territory. Chitwood could easily reach the Yellow Sea, but if he couldn't air start his 86, he was in for one long and very cold swim. Fortunately, the engine restarted and Chitwood returned to K-13.

Harold Chitwood is awarded the DFC after completing his 100th mission.

Following his combat tour, Chitwood was posted to Nellis as an instructor pilot. One afternoon while teaching an 86-student pilot how to make a dead-stick landing, the fire-warning light in Chitwood's jet flashed on. He knew he'd have to shut down his engine immediately so he climbed quickly, killed his engine, and entered the traffic pattern as a glider, putting it down softly on the runway.

On another occasion, Chitwood was flying a T-33 some seventy-five miles from the base when his engine quit. The silence of an inoperable engine really is deafening. Chitwood made three attempts at a restart and the engine caught, but on all three occasions when power was reapplied, the engine quit once more. Chitwood was now flying a glider once again, a very heavy glider. It was time to lighten the aircraft, so he dropped his wing tanks. One rolled up over the wing and lodged itself against the vertical stabilizer. Here was a volatile fuel tank begging to blow up. Chitwood prepared to bail out but before doing so decided to roll the T-33 and see if it might help. It did, the tank fell free, and Chitwood entered the pattern and completed a perfect dead-stick landing.

When Chitwood's engine quit seventy-five miles from his base, he dropped his wing tanks. One of them damaged his horizontal stabilizer.

Perhaps Chitwood tired of flying gliders or landing powerless planes, or perhaps he looked forward to a nine-to-five job. Whatever the reason, he retired from the Air Force and joined the Gold Kist Poultry Company, which processed some 15,000,000 chickens per week. Thirty years later he was named its CEO. How appropriate—throughout his entire Air Force career, whether he was in cadets, combat, or instructing at Nellis, Harold Chitwood played chicken time and time again, and time and time again he won.

Ben Gilmore Goes Ape in Korea

Silk scarf, sunglasses, moustache, flight jacket...Ben Gilmore must have been on his way to central casting.

Ben Gilmore decided he'd make a better pilot than a student. Rice Institute helped him make that decision by flunking him out of school, which was not the high point in his career. Gilmore enlisted in aviation cadets and was posted to Greenville with the class of 52-Charlie. Initially, Gilmore fared no better at Greenville than at

Rice. He went swimming in the base pool and came down with an ear infection. The flight surgeon treated the infection by pouring ether into his ear.

"It was the most intense pain I ever experienced," Gilmore reported. Apparently flight surgeons have better luck when they stick to prescribing eight ounces of liquor.

In the next few weeks things didn't get much better. The day he soloed he was shooting crosswind landings, when a gust of wind lifted his starboard wing and pushed his T-6 onto the grass. He distinctly remembers hearing his instructor screaming instructions at him from the back seat, which was unusual as the back seat was empty! Gilmore hit his brakes, his rudders, and everything else he found in the cockpit and eventually returned his plane to the runway. He avoided ground looping the T-6, but he managed to cover the wing tips with grass stains. Gilmore received the same grade for his first solo effort as he did for his final exam at Rice, but he did graduate from primary and was sent to Reese AFB for advanced training in B-25s. Gilmore was delighted. The B-25 had a tricycle landing gear, which made it virtually impossible to ground loop the plane. But the day after he arrived, he was told he would complete his training in the T-6. His luck had not changed.

After six more months of flying the T-6, Gilmore graduated from cadets and was sent to Wichita to check out in the F-80. On his first solo takeoff, Gilmore stalled out and barely avoided destroying his aircraft. Fortunately, his F-80 bounced off the gears' shock absorbers, which gave him enough elevation to complete the takeoff. His instructor pilot watched the whole procedure, shaking his head.

Wichita was glad to send Gilmore on to Nellis to check out in the F-86. One morning, his instructor pilot leaned into the cockpit of an 86, started the engine, and said to Ben, "Take it up and see how you like it."

Gilmore had flown only a few hours in an 86 simulator. This was not a simulator. It was a big airplane with a powerful engine. Gilmore told me if he had known how to shut off the engine, he would've done so and returned to civilian life. But he didn't, so he got in the 86 and taxied to the runway. Ben fell in love that day. With the F-86!

Nellis was a gunnery school. Pilots would practice high-angle strafing. The tower would control the pattern, which began at 10,000 feet. Each pilot would make a steep turn, dive, sight the target, fire and pull back to 10,000 feet, executing a sloppy Immelman on the way. The bent-wing 86, however, did not pull out of a dive like the 80 or the T-6. It mushed. Several pilots were killed because they focused on the target too long and failed to pull out in time.

Next stop, K-13 for a combat stint. On his first familiarization flight, Gilmore toured South Korea, rubbernecking from 20,000 feet, and let time get away from him. When he returned to the base, an emergency was declared and the tower closed the runway. Gilmore's fuel now could be measured with an eyedropper and his prospects were not bright.

Luck was Gilmore's co-pilot that day. He landed safely. But as he turned off the runway, his engine quit, so he contacted the tower, "Tower, this is AF 123. I'm out of fuel."

The tower immediately broadcast an emergency message, alerting all the other aircraft in the vicinity that an 86 was in trouble and the pattern was closed. The tower then asked Gilmore, "What's your altitude? Where are you located?"

"Right below you. I'm parked below the tower." Needless to say, the tower was not amused.

Gilmore flew only twelve combat missions in Korea, but in that time, he was attacked by a MiG and shot at by ground forces. After his brief combat tour, Gilmore was transferred to intelligence duties in Japan, which seemed an odd assignment for someone who had flunked out of college.

Perhaps the hallmark of Gilmore's flying career began on an R & R when some line soldiers gave him a monkey named "Ace." Ace was a constant companion, and Gilmore even took him up in a C-47. It turned out Ace was a borderline alcoholic. Gilmore's friends got him drunk in the officers' club on a night when an air raid alert was called.

The officers donned their helmets and ran to their battle stations. Ace turned his water can upside down, strapped it to his head, and danced around his cage.

Gilmore spent five-and-a-half years in the Air Force and reached the rank of captain. Then the man who flunked out of Rice went back to college and earned a degree in mechanical engineering and industrial engineering and was the first SMU engineering student accepted in the MBA program at Harvard Business School. The intelligence service must have known something others didn't.

Ben Gilmore loved every minute of the time he served his country. He was shot at. He was chased by a MIG, flew America's hottest jet, spent time at the Yalu River, and got drunk with a monkey named Ace. What else could he ask for?

Gilmore has just returned from a combat mission and is looking forward to the officers' club and a beer with his monkey.

Three Wars—243 Combat Missions and Not a Scratch

Don Stewart had 112 combat missions in Korea, flew with two of America's leading aces, and was credited with a MiG.

Don Stewart joined the merchant marine in June of 1944 at the age of seventeen and worked as a fireman on a tanker sailing the Atlantic at a time when the German U-boats were active. After his service at sea, Stewart decided he'd prefer to fly over the sea rather than sail on it, so he transferred to the Air Force and applied for pilot training. He completed his basic training at Greenville, his advanced training at Williams and then was posted to K-14 in Korea for his first combat tour. There his flight commander was Manuel (Pete) Fernandez, the third-ranking ace in Korea, and one hell of a combat pilot. The second-ranking ace, Jabarra, was the squadron exec. Stewart flew with both these men and that can be good, or it can be bad. If you are flying with an ace, rest assured you will seek out the enemy and engage at every opportunity. One day, his group of four 86s encountered sixteen MiGs and all hell broke loose. His flight commander, Pete Fernandez, was as cool as a cucumber. He directed his group through the fight, shooting down a MiG in the process while Stewart stayed as close to Fernandez as his flying skills allowed.

Most of the Stewart's missions took him north to the Yalu and his responsibility was to protect Hernandez, not shoot at MiGs. Once Fernandez completed his tour, Stewart took over and was credited with at least one MiG damaged.

Following the Korean fracas, Stewart became an instructor in the Air Defense Command Interceptor Weapons School. In 1958, he graduated from Air Force Test Pilot School at Edwards AFB and became an operational test pilot and test director at Tyndall AFB, where he had the pleasure of checking out two former Korean aces: Col. James Johnson and the legendary "Grey Eagle," Vermont Garrison, who had ten kills in WW II and another ten in Korea.

In June 1970, Stewart was assigned command of the 34th Tactical Fighter Squadron at Karats AFB in Thailand and flew the F-4E Phantom jet on 131 combat missions, targeting buildings, bridges, tanks, trucks, the Ho Chi Min Trail, enemy troops, and equipment. Most of his missions bottomed out below 5,000 feet and were met with 23, 37, and 57 mm cannon shells. His luck held out. He was never hit, never in the 243 combat missions he flew in Korea and Vietnam.

Don Stewart spent twenty-nine years in the service, earning a chestful of medals including the Legion of Merit, four Distinguished Flying Crosses, and thirteen Air Medals. In addition, he has service ribbons from every theater of operations, the Atlantic, the Pacific, and the Mediterranean.

Don Stewart retired a full colonel with an impeccable combat record, a history of teaching and testing, and about 4,500 hours in the air with not a scratch on his body.

Stewart flew 243 combat missions. He was not happy unless someone was shooting at him.

White Light, Red Fire

Before they converted to night flying, B-29s were shot down on virtually every mission. After the F-94 night fighter became operational, only occasionally was a B-29 lost. Still, it was a terrible moment when good friends became statistics and faces slowly dissolved as memories distilled.

Most of the missions I flew in January and February were uncontested but the minute I walked into the briefing room on March 15, 1953, I sensed that was about to change. The room was filled with pilots, navigators, bombardiers, and radar operators. The mood was tentative. The light-hearted raillery that normally masked our true feelings was missing. There had been rumors, rumors about what part of hell we would be visiting in the next twelve hours.

We were seated facing a stage with a large screen and an overhead projector. A major paced back and forth on the stage carrying a yardstick, which he nervously tapped on the floor.

"Attention!" he screamed in a falsetto voice as Lieutenant Colonel Larkin entered the briefing room.

We rose as one and stood rigidly at attention. Larkin was respected by his men, even loved by them. The colonel strode the length of the stage, peering into the soul of every young officer in the room. He knew each of the seventy-five men by name, by reputation, by pride.

"Be seated," he ordered pleasantly. "Gentlemen, our targets tonight are the bridges at Sinanju. The spring floods have begun, and if we can take out a few bridges in the next few days, we'll shove a plug up their supply lines that'll save one hell of a lot of American lives. There is a problem, however. This will be the third night in a row that these bridges have been bombed and the gooks know exactly the short range, navigational (shoran) arc we will be flying. They have set up high-intensity lights along the arc. They will be fixed, so ECM will be useless. Approaching the target they have more triple-A (antiaircraft artillery) than you will find in all of North Korea. As you approach bombs away, you will have to fly through a bowl of searchlights. Antiaircraft will cease and in that bowl will be a squadron of MiGs with their 37-millimeter cannons. Get in, drop your bombs, and get out as quickly as you can. Make 'em count, because we don't want to go back. Triple A's going to be heavy and we're going to see some of Russia's best tonight. Godspeed."

Godspeed indeed! The expressions on the officers' faces leaving the briefing room attested to the fact that this was not going to be a pleasant night. Darkness was the only shield we had against the MiG-15. What they couldn't see, they couldn't hit. But tonight, we would be lit up like a Christmas tree and it was virtually certain that we would lose at least one plane.

I remember how dry my mouth was as I left the briefing room and headed to route and target study. I heard very little there. I was already over the target staring into the white lights that burst up from the ground twenty thousand feet below. So far my combat experience was a walk in the park; I had not seen the burst of an antiaircraft shell or watched a golden 37 mm cannon tracer shell arch its way over an aircraft. So far it was all fun and games. That would end tonight.

The army truck dropped our crew off at the hard stand. In the gathering darkness, our 29 was silhouetted against the evening sky, its bomb bays yawning with safety tags hanging from its lethal load of 500-pound bombs. A black mat was spread by the nose of the aircraft and eleven parachutes placed carefully on top. We put on our chutes and stood in a line so each man's chute could be inspected by the airman behind him. Pins were checked and adjusted.

And then a small green cart was pushed in front of the aircraft. I was convinced it was a tumbrel left over from the French revolution. Inside were flak jackets. Each member of the crew selected a piece of body armor...just in case.

The bombardier went to the bomb bays and pulled the safety tags from the forty bombs. They were now live, ten tons of bombs.

We boarded the aircraft, started the engines, and awaited instructions from the tower to taxi to the active runway behind the 29 in front of us.

There a green light flashed.

Smith touched my arm and said, "You got it, Lieutenant."

"Roger."

I pushed the throttles forward while holding the brakes firmly. When the throttles reached the firewall, I released the brakes. The heavily laden 29 lumbered down the runway and lifted gently into the darkening sky.

My mouth was dry. My hands were wet. And I remember singing to myself, "Yellow Polka Dot Bikini."

The B-29 carries a crew of eleven: four gunners, a radio operator, a flight engineer, a navigator, a radar operator, a bombardier, and two pilots. The bombardier was a supernumerary, just along for the ride. The radar operator dropped our bombs by guiding the aircraft down a short-range navigational arc until it crossed a second arc where the bombs were automatically released. The arcs were created by two radio beams broadcast from stations near the front line. Our radar operator was one of the best in the squadron. He could drop a donut in a cup of coffee from twenty thousand feet.

On the way to the target, the gunners tested their guns. Tonight there seemed to be intensity to the test fire that I had not heard before. Eleven men sat back and watched the ocean disappear far below their aircraft, waiting, praying.

"Ten minutes to the IP," the navigator called out.

In the distance we could see the searchlights reaching up to catch a 29 in its beam. As we got closer, the whole sky lit up and the few clouds below us became filaments for the bright lights far below. Lazy puffs of black smoke dotted the horizon and turned the smooth night air into a turbulent sea. The black puffs continued as we bumped our way toward the target.

"IP!"

"Roger. Open the bomb bay doors!"

"Doors open."

"Radar, it's your aircraft."

"Roger, I got it," Lieutenant Sharp replied.

Captain Smith and I took our hands off the controls and for twenty seconds we could take no evasive action. If we were hit, so be it.

Just ahead we saw the bowl of lights and then we were in it. I had the feeling I was sitting on top of a large teacup looking down into a valley of light and fire. The black puffs had disappeared but a golden ball of fire arched gently over the B-29 just ahead of us. A benign-looking form of instant death. The lights were so bright I could read the numbers on the plane's tail surfaces.

Than another golden ball. And another.

"Ten seconds to bombs away."

A MiG-15 screamed silently across the bow of my aircraft and then another and another. Tracers from their guns arced toward a B-29 flying just to our right. No doubt some of those tracers found their mark, but the 29 plowed on.

This was the only night I would hear the reports of our guns firing as our CFC (central-fire-control) aimed at the MiGs darting about like fireflies at a picnic.

"Five seconds."

Five seconds is an eternity when you know the next fireball may kill every man on your plane. As soon as the radar operator called, "Bombs away!" Smith made a diving turn to get out of the search-lights. As he did, we could see the muzzle flashes of antiaircraft guns on the ground. This was the longest five minutes of my life, yet I remember feeling calm and unconcerned as the whole sky exploded around our 29. I wasn't the only one. Not one member of the crew evidenced any fear.

One by one the searchlights switched off and the MIGs returned to their safe haven in Manchuria. One by one the 29s began their long journey home to Japan or Okinawa. One by one the members of the crews sat back in their seats and reflected on just how lucky they had been and wondered if there was a 29 that would not be returning to its base this night.

The dawn rose slowly over a cloudless sky like a breath of fresh oxygen, creeping ever so slowly above a waveless ocean. The tip of South Korea disappeared off our stern and war was once again a thousand light years away.

Peaceful. The serenity of the ocean below, of the sky, of the carmine-red sun beginning to obscure the popcorn-yellow moon as it set in the west.

The engineer checked the cylinder-head temperatures. The navigator shot the stars and assured me that we were on course but behind schedule.

Then a small speck interrupted the endless sea, an island. My island.

It had been ten hours to hell and back and now it was less than ten minutes to a runway.

Flaps at fifteen, mixtures rich, full RPM. Final approach, gear down, flaps to forty-five. We were five hundred feet from the best-looking patch of cement I'd ever seen.

The soft screech of tires touching a cement runway can be the most reassuring sound in the world. We guided the plane to the end of the runway and then on to our hard stand. I joined my crewmembers on the tarmac where we embraced each other and all the while, the lyrics of "Yellow Polka Dot Bikini" pounded in my head.

There would be empty bunks in Kadena that night, and new airmen would soon be assigned those bunks. Nothing had changed. The hard stands were refilled, the five-hundred-pound bombs still had yellow-painted noses, the endless line of copper shell casings glistened in the moonlight, and the river that passed through Sinanju was clogged with bits of broken bridges and stray pieces of a B-29.

Mutiny on the 774

Our plane had suffered minor damage in the mission over Sinanju, enough to ground 774 until repairs were made. So we had time on our hands.

Every man has his own way of dealing with the pressures of war. Some prefer to be alone. Some would rather be around friends, talking, joking, laughing. If a plane had been lost, few talked about the missing crew. They would not be mourned but they would be remembered, and only the good memories would be retained.

I dealt with pressure differently than most. After we landed and were debriefed, three officers from the crew met in my hut, cooked bacon and eggs over a propane stove and played cribbage.

We were exhausted, barely able to keep our eyes open. We'd not been to bed for thirty-six hours, but adrenalin ruled and we were riding an emotional high. The game lasted for a little over two hours before each officer returned to his quarters and went to sleep for the next fifteen hours.

When we were not flying combat, we spent most of our evenings at the officers' club, where I occasionally entertained with piano selections I had written about the service. During Easter, I wrote, produced, and emceed a show to raise money for the March of Dimes. Military personnel are the most generous people I know. We raised more than three thousand dollars that one evening and I had a ball.

For just a while the war was forgotten. But the minute I strapped on a parachute, the pressure returned.

Three days after the raid on Sinanju, 774 was ready to be test flown.

Lieutenant Gushee entertains at the March of Dimes benefit in Okinawa

It was a beautiful April morning, with soft white stratus clouds stretching to the horizon. We checked our parachutes and boarded the plane. Captain Smith taxied 774 to the runway. He was a fine pilot. He had more than a thousand hours, most of which was accumulated flying extremely hazardous missions in WW II.

We took off, climbed to seven thousand feet, and completed all the checks our maintenance officer required. We lowered and raised the gear, opened and closed the bomb bay doors, reduced power on each engine and activated the transfer pumps, raised and lowered the flaps, and tested the hydraulic system. 774 flew like an angel.

Suddenly Smith cried out, "Goddamn it, engineer, I have no air speed. My indicator registers zero."

"Mine too!" the navigator said, bending around the forward turret and thrusting his face into the cockpit.

"Mine's working," I reassured Smith. "Engineer, how's your air speed indicator?"

"Okay, sir."

Many of the systems in the B-29 are redundant for safety reasons. There are two pitot tubes that measure air speed. The airplane commander's and the navigator's work from one, the co-pilot's and engineer's from the other.

"We're okay, Captain," I said.

"Bullshit!" he screamed. "If we get into clouds we'll all be killed!"

Captain Smith had made a terrible mistake. He panicked, and when he did he forgot to turn off his throat mike. Everyone in the aft of the aircraft heard him and lined up at the rear hatch in preparation for bailing out. All they had to do was look outside. We couldn't get back to the base without flying through a cloud deck, and according to the captain, if we got into clouds we were going to die.

"We are in no danger!" I announced over the interphone. "Take your positions and relax. That's an order."

I landed the aircraft as Smith sat in his seat staring out the window.

That night, the officers of the crew came to my bungalow. They were a somber lot. Our navigator, who was the highest-ranking member of our crew, initiated the conversation, "Lieutenant, we've decided we will no longer fly with Captain Smith. He's a dangerous man. We want you to go to Command and request a new airplane commander."

"Why me, Major? I'm the lowest-ranking officer on the crew."

"You know why, Lieutenant. When it comes to matters of the aircraft, you are number two. You outrank us here. It's your responsibility."

"Do you know what you are? You are mutineers and you know what they do to mutineers during war, they shoot them. I don't like flying with Smith anymore than you do but I intend to come out of this war with my body intact. I will assure you that if we get into a situation Smith cannot handle, I'll take over. You have my promise on that. I will not let the man endanger our lives."

Lieutenant Sharp thought for a moment and responded, "You are right, Lieutenant, I withdraw my request. I can however ask to be transferred to another crew, can I not?"

"Yes, you can, but the chances are slim that Command will act on your request. The wing is desperately short of personnel. Have any of you talked to the enlisted men about this?"

"Yes, we have," Captain Dudendorf said. "They feel the same way."

"Well, I suggest you tell them about our conversation and assure them that the situation will be handled.

"And before we break off, let me say one more thing. We have known from the moment we met that our captain left a lot to be desired. Yet we have flown fifteen combat missions and are ranked among the top crews in the wing, with a bottle of whiskey to show for it. Like him or not, Smith's a fine pilot. Think about that before you hurry to wing with a request for a crew change. If it makes any difference, I happen to like flying with you bastards."

One grows up quickly in a war. A mutiny had been averted and in a strange way we were a much stronger crew for it.

Maximum Effort

Waldo Cecil has some bridges to bomb and some dams to breach.

The bridges at Sinanju and the surrounding reservoirs and dams were the most important targets in North Korea. Supplies from the north could not reach the front lines without going over a bridge in Sinanju. If the bridges were knocked out, those supplies were endangered. Every resource we had was brought to bear in an effort to knock those bridges out, including B-29s from Japan and Okinawa and fighter/bombers from bases in South Korea.

The bridges at Sinanju were the targets of a maximum effort in January and again in April. And the reservoir dams got the nod in May. During a maximum effort, every available plane is assigned to fly.

In January, the F-84s from K-8 joined those from K-2. Each plane flew three missions a day for three days. Nine missions per aircraft, saturation bombing. The ordnance dropped on the bridges at Sinanju defies description. The job was done, but at a cost.

Waldo Cecil, 52-Charlie, was part of that maximum effort. Cecil graduated from Bryan AFB and after gunnery training at Luke, he was sent directly to K-2 to fly 84s. The pilots who flew those missions will never forget them. The MiGs dove into their own flak in order to disrupt the dive-bombers. Black puffs of death were everywhere and orange balls of cannon fire from the MiGs added a surreal patina to the carnage.

John Pentecost, 52-C, and a good friend of Cecil's from K-8, participated in the Sinanju attacks. At the end of the first day, there was a snowstorm at K-8 and Pentecost and his flight had to land at K-2 and remain over night there. Pentecost bunked with Cecil, and the two pilots spent most of that night talking about their combat experiences. The next morning it was back to work, back to Sinanju for a second day.

Each 84 approached Sinanju from 25,000 to 30,000 feet. As they neared the target, they began their letdown, with flights of four forming up in trail to provide space for each pilot to roll onto the target, one behind the other. They began their run at altitudes ranging from 7,500 to 11,000 feet. On the bomb run, the F-84 reached a speed in excess of 400 knots. The pilots released their bombs at 2000 feet, which was the most dangerous part of the mission. They could take no evasive action and it appeared as though every gun in North Korea fired on them. Cecil was hit by shards of an antiaircraft shell. "It sounded like someone was throwing gravel at the canopy."

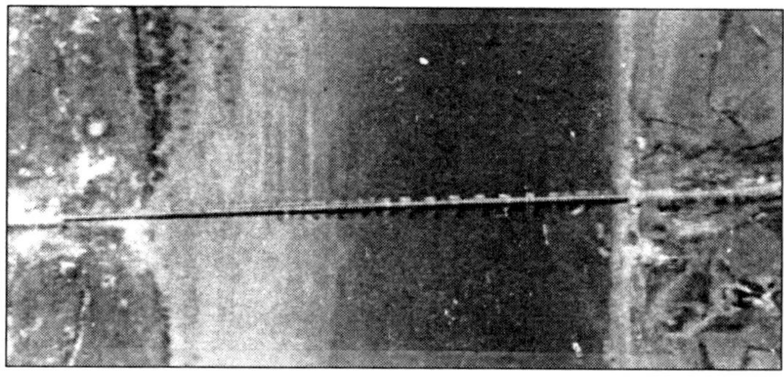

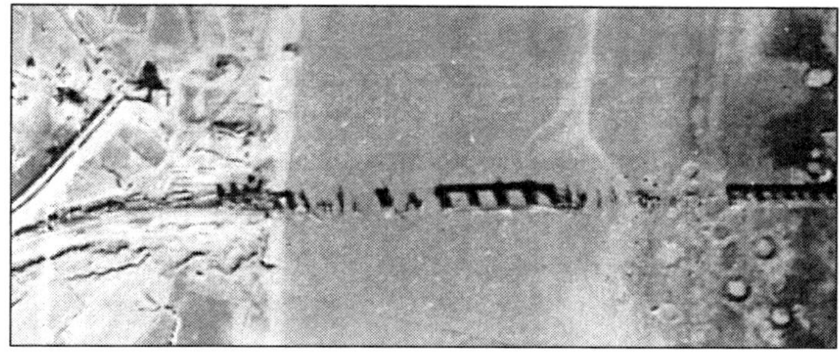

Before and after: 9 spans destroyed, 3 direct hits, and a whole lot of men and materials that didn't get to the South for a while.

Cecil heard a pilot describe how one member of his group lost a wing to ground fire, snap-rolled and dove straight into the ground. The pilot was John Pentecost and he didn't have a chance.

By April the bridges had been rebuilt and it was time to hit them again. An ideal time because the spring floods would make it difficult to rebuild them. The North Koreans knew exactly from what direction the F-84s and the B-29s would fly over the target. They placed their guns and lights along this line. The pilots could not avoid the guns and at night the bombers could not avoid the searchlights. The mission was successful, but American planes and American pilots were lost.

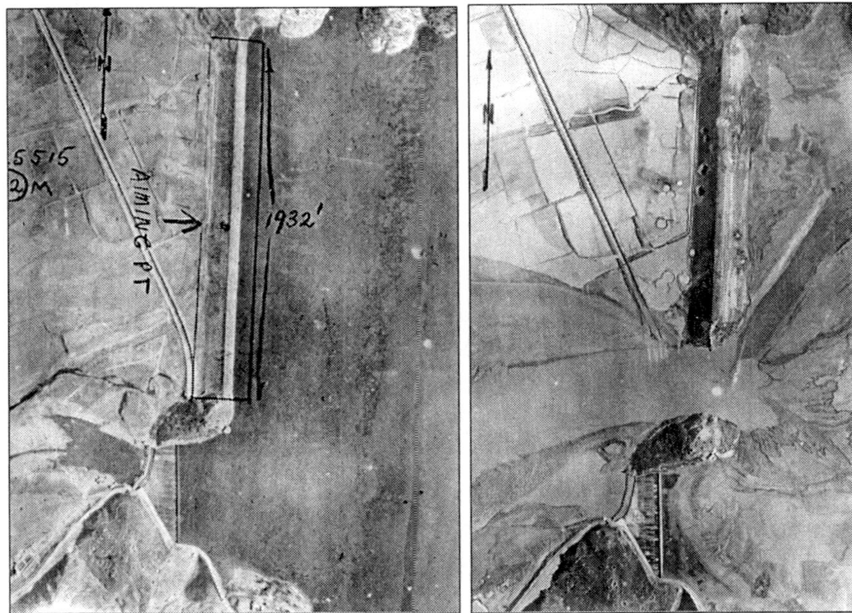

The Toksan Dam—before and after: 88 buildings, an airfield, a high-tension tower, and roadways were destroyed and a large area was flooded.

Almost as important were a series of reservoir dams. The largest was the Toksan Dam. On May 13 Cecil flew three missions against the Toksan as flight leader. By the end of the day, the 58th Fighter Bomber wing had more than forty hits on the dam. Upon returning the next morning to finish it off, they found the dam had breached during the night, flooding the area, and causing extensive damage.

Ten days later another reservoir was targeted. The North Koreans had anticipated this and moved every gun from the Toksan area to this site. It bristled with guns. The mission leader was John Addison, 52-C. Cecil led the second flight behind Addison. As Cecil rolled onto the target, he saw a cascade of what appeared to be aluminum foil, followed by a large explosion some 400 yards to the left of the target. He assumed that Addison's number four had crashed, but that was not the case. An 84 had been hit, but it was still flying. Cecil cut his power and pulled alongside the stricken 84 pilot, Roger Daniels, who was in shock. It took several seconds to get Daniels to respond. His first words were, “I can’t get much airspeed and a panel light shows my nose wheel is down. Can you check?”

The entire lower portion of the fuselage had been blown away, including the nose gear, the fuel tank, the tip tank, and a portion of the leading edge of the wing.

Cecil didn’t want to alarm Daniels so he said, “Your gear’s not down, don’t worry about it.”

A line drawing of Roger Daniels’ F-84...No gear, no tip tank, torn wing. Still

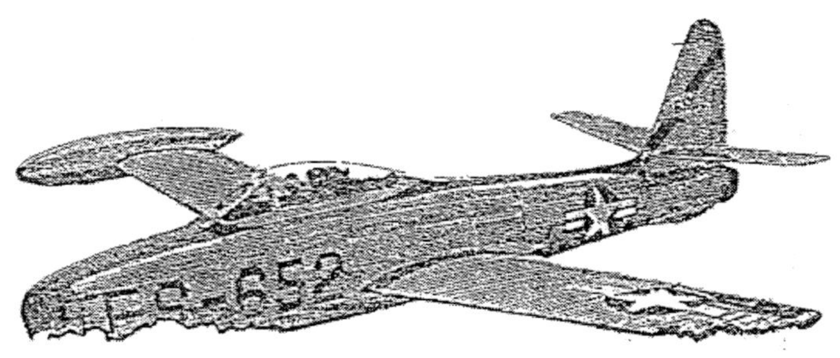

it flew Daniels to safety.

Daniels couldn’t make it back to the base with his plane, so Cecil gave him a heading to the west coast, where the UN maintained a small island with rescue potential. Cecil called RESCAP flight for assistance and alerted a chopper. The most direct flight path to the island would take the two planes over Pyongyang and subject them to heavy antiaircraft fire. Daniels’ plane was in such poor shape he couldn’t divert around the city. The two pilots had to fly directly over Pyongyang. Cecil zigzagged his aircraft to draw attention away from Daniels. Neither plane was hit by flak. When they reached the coast, contact was made with the chopper. Daniels bailed out and watched his 84 plunge into the ocean. He was picked up in less than a minute and a tragedy was averted.

Waldo Cecil’s Korean experiences did not end there. He continued to fly combat, including many close support missions. On one such mission, he and his flight of four aircraft were directed to the Punch Bowl to go spelunking with Bill Harrington, a Mosquito pilot and member of 52-Charlie.

Their target that day was a mobile gun that was hidden in a cave and was raising hell with our troops. They tried circling the area at about 5000 feet in order to pick out the target. But AAA was so intense the flight had to climb to 7500 feet and the shadows of the mountain made it impossible to locate the cave. The only way to approach it was to fly down a valley to get a dead shot on the target.

Harrington was asked to mark the target with "Willie Peter" rockets. This he did amidst very heavy flak and tracers. Cecil's flight could not believe that Harrington made it through that run without being shot down. Harrington fired a few of his rockets, but Cecil couldn't see where they landed. He asked a wary Harrington to repeat the run and told him that he'd fall in behind his plane.

Harrington was not a happy camper, but he did as he was asked and put two rockets right into the cave. Each plane in Waldo's flight carried two one-thousand-pound bombs. They each made two passes at the cave and at least one bomb went into the mouth of the cave, sealing it with the gun inside.

The happiest man in the flight? Bill Harrington. He wanted no part of a third run down that valley. Two members of 52-C, working together, saved many American lives that day.

In 1991, some 38 years later, Waldo Cecil met a retired army colonel who had witnessed this mission. The colonel told Cecil that it was the most impressive bit of flying he had ever seen.

When Waldo Cecil retired he wore a chestful of ribbons and medals including two DFCs and a flock of air medals. He had been an integral part of one of the few Maximum Efforts flown during the Korean War; he helped direct an American pilot to safety; he destroyed a gun emplacement that was killing UN troops by the score; and he did it without concern for his own well being.

Cecil returned to civilian life and as the manager of manufacturing at Texas Plastics he helped design and produce an over-visor for

Why are these men smiling? They are Lieutenant Baker and Lieutenant Cecil and they have just completed their 100 missions. They are on their way home.

Ed White to use when he became the first man to walk in space on his historic Gemini 4 flight, which was commanded by another member of 52-Charlie, astronaut Jim McDivitt.

Never Volunteer

Ray Kelly...all smiles. This was before he took a 37 mm shell in his dive doors.

For as long as there has been a military there has been an unwritten rule: Never volunteer! And for as long as that rule has existed, it has seldom been honored. There's something about members of the military. When asked, their hands shoot up faster than the eye can record.

Ray Kelly was one of the members of 52-Charlie who broke that rule and it almost cost him his life. Kelly scored hits on the dams two days in a row and was scheduled to fly one more mission against the dams with Bob Anderson, one hell of a pilot who later flew with the Thunderbirds. When the two men reached their target, they found the dams had been breached, so they selected an alternate target, dropped their bombs, and returned to the base.

Kelly got in his relaxing clothes and went to the card room. After a few minutes the squadron officer came in looking for volunteers. The engine of an enemy train had been destroyed, but the boxcars it was pulling were stuck on a track near Pyongyang and OPS wanted those cars bombed. It sounded like a milk run and it counted as a combat mission.

Anderson, Kelly, and two other card players volunteered. They drew straws for who would lead and who would fly numbers 2, 3, and 4. Anderson won and off they went. Kelly remembers he was wearing low top-dress shoes, which weren't exactly government issue for a combat mission.

The target was a sitting duck. It was going to be a day at a shooting gallery. But as it turned out, it was a trap. The Koreans had placed guns all around the boxcars. All four planes went in on the deck and Anderson and one other member of the flight dropped their bombs on the boxcars. Kelly was not so fortunate. As he released his bombs, he took a 37 mm shell in the dive door and all hell broke loose. He lost his aileron boost, which meant he had to manually control the flight surfaces. That took both hands on the stick.

The fire-warning light glowed red in Kelly's cockpit. Anderson told Kelly his plane was on fire and recommended he bail out. But Kelly couldn't get over the fact he was wearing improper shoes and therefore he shouldn't bail out. It's strange what goes through one's mind at a moment like this. Kelly had his dress shoes on and that changed everything. He also noticed he was flying over a POW camp at Pyongyang and he had no intention of bailing out over a POW camp.

Kelly pulled back on the stick to gain altitude, and when he reached 6000 feet the fire-warning light went off. Kelly assumed the fire had gone out and indeed it had. He still wasn't out of the woods. He could pull only 80 per cent power, which wasn't going to keep him in the air long. He couldn't make it back to his base; in fact, he'd be lucky to reach the coast and a friendly beach. But it was worth a try. In the meantime, every AAA gun in Pyongyang started shooting at him. The sky was filled with black. Anderson and the other members of Kelly's flight were at 30,000 feet, safely out of reach, and yelling encouraging words to their wingman.

Kelly kept his 84 in the air and reached the coast, where the rescue helicopter ordered him to bail out, but he wasn't of a mind to jump into the sea at that moment. His plane was under control and there was an island, Paengnyongdo, with a 5000-foot sand beach used for emergency landings. Kelly told the rescue 'copter to follow him down.

He prepared for his final approach and received his second unwanted surprise; his dive brakes and flaps were useless, which meant a hot landing. Kelly touched down at 200 knots and when his nose wheel hit the beach it collapsed. Fortunately the plane came to a stop without any further incident. He got out of his 84 amidst the shout-

The Fighting Kellys...Richard Kelly, Hank Kelly, Ray Kelly, all pilots in the 69th FBS K-2, Korea. Related only by the planes they flew.

ing of ground personnel asking him to hurry it up. The tide was coming in and if they didn't recover the plane within an hour it would be under water. Ray Kelly had seen enough of that 84 and didn't give a damn if it sank to the bottom of the ocean. Island personnel managed to lift the plane off the sand before the tide came in.

Kelly had several shots of the medics' finest whiskey and spent the night on the island in a tent. That island is a very popular game resort today.

Ray Kelly continued to fly combat, completing 102 missions including two with the Mosquito Squadron before rotating back to the States. He enjoyed his experiences in Korea and learned one very valuable lesson: Never, never volunteer!

Yalu Fever

A few weeks after our mission over Sinanju we were reminded that this was not a war, this was a police action, and there were rules, rules that allowed our enemy sanctuaries from whence they could attack us and be impervious to attack by us. There were airfields like Antung in Manchuria and the Suiho Dam on the Yalu River that were off-limits. If we had been allowed to destroy the Suiho Dam it would have flooded the valley and turned off the lights of two major North Korean cities and one major military base. But we were told the dam was owned by a member country of the United Nations, so it was taboo.

As was Antung, a city in Manchuria. President Truman didn't want to widen the war, so Manchuria was also off-limits. But not to the Russians or the Chinese, who were fighting the same war. This was their safe haven. They were so bold as to turn their runway lights on at night while their MiGs took off with wing lights blazing. The Chinese used Antung as the base from which they shot down American planes and interrogated UN prisoners of war. They supplied the North Koreans with every armament they needed. We couldn't drop a water balloon on Antung without the White House castigating the commanders at Kadena.

War is hell on an even playing field, but when the rules differ for each side, war is inhuman. This unfortunately was a lesson we learned in Korea, which we repeated in Vietnam and once again in Iraq, where no one seems to object when terrorists behead their prisoners, but if we ridicule a POW we are held up to scorn throughout the world.

Fight wars with rules or fight them without rules, but be consistent.

There were times when I actually thought we were in a war, not a police action, times like the few moments we spent over Sinanju or when we watched a friend's aircraft blow up, or we listened to the story of Quinn Fuller's first combat mission.

Tonight I would once again be reminded that this was a push-button war and all the buttons were in Washington, D.C.

Servicemen have an extraordinary talent for sensing when a dangerous mission is scheduled, even before that mission is announced. One can see it in their walk, their eyes, their faces, long before it is confirmed in a briefing room.

"Sinuiju," the captain said, pointing to a spot on the map by the Yalu River. "Sinuiju is our target for tonight. Unfortunately, the moon will be full and it will be up all night."

We might as well be flying a daylight mission. We would be silhouetted against the moon, easy prey for MiGs. We would need all the F-94s the fighter boys could launch.

Three Russian pilots, Suckov, Oskin, and Snorchkov, had shot down seven B-29s and Anatoly Karelin had shot down six B-29s by himself, all at night. These were excellent pilots, and despite what the Kremlin claimed, they were in Korea, and they flew combat.

The briefing continued. Coordinates were given along with the admonition that if our bombs did not automatically release, we were to go on to the secondary target.

"UNDER NO CIRCUSTANCES ARE YOU TO PICKLE YOUR BOMBS ON ANTUNG. THAT, GENTLEMEN, IS A PRESIDENTIAL ORDER."

There is nothing that screams so loud as total silence. There was not a sound in the room, not a finger moved, not a toe or an eyelash. Moments passed before any of the seventy-five officers breathed. Tonight there was no false bravado, no jokes, no conversation. Seventy-five mummies exited the briefing room and walked solemnly to route and target study.

Our target was just a few short miles from the Chinese base at Antung, at the northernmost point of North Korea. This was to be the deepest penetration we would have as a crew and we'd spend more than an hour flying over enemy territory in the bright light of a full moon.

The bus dropped our crew off at the hard stand and I began my walk around, checking the sumps and going through the motions of checking the surfaces. My thoughts were a thousand miles away.

We lined up in a row so that each crew member could have his parachute checked by the man behind him. Were the pins in straight? Were the flaps closed tightly? Was there any chute showing? And all the while each man prayed to God that he would never have to use it.

Captain Dudendorf pulled the safety tags from the 500-pouind bombs in the bomb bay. The gunners entered the aircraft. I made one final check, pulled myself up through the nose-wheel hatch, and strapped myself into the righthand seat. Smith and I completed the preflight checklist and it was time to start engines.

The crew chief pointed to the number three engine and twirled his hand. The flight engineer switched on the magneto and I started the engine. Engines number two, one, and four followed. A light from the tower flashed through the windows above us and Smith slowly inched the throttles forward to begin our taxi to the runway.

Fifteen B-29s make one hell of a lot of noise, but when your gut is telling you that you may not make sunrise, you don't hear a whisper.

Another light flashed and a 29 lumbered down the ten-thousand-foot unlit runway struggling to lift its load of death off Kadena, followed by a second, then a third 29.

It was now our turn. Smith poured the coal to the engines and soon we became a part of the bright night sky. The drone of the engines over an unseen ocean was soporific. I found it almost impossible to keep my eyes open. Yet there was much to be done. The gunners must test the guns. The radar operator had to check the ECM equipment, the engineer must balance the fuel in the wing tanks, and the navigator must be certain we arrived over the target with a one-minute separation from the other B-29s in the formation. I was responsible for flying the plane and making damn sure we didn't hit another B-29 along the way.

When we reached the tip of Korea we turned to our assigned radio frequency. There was activity that night we had not heard since we flew against Sinanju. Night-flying F-94s were being called in by other bomber wings to chase away the MiGs. The skies over North Korea were busy and bright and it did not bode well.

We crossed the front lines and I addressed the crew.

"Gentlemen, we are now in enemy territory, and we will be here for at least an hour, so keep your eyes peeled. The moon is up and we're dangling in the sky like a Christmas ornament. If you see an aircraft let me know. If you think it's a MiG clear your guns, but don't fire until I give you permission." Having said that, I told the crew that there was not a lot of activity on the command set. "I think the bastards are taking the night off. It's going to be a walk in the park."

I lied. I knew this was going to be ticklish, but why get the gunners upset? There was nothing they could do about it. My words had the desired effect. Some of the strain in the cockpit eased.

More chatter on the radio. The moonlight glistened off our wing, but there was no sign of the enemy. Not yet.

Time walks on weighted feet when fear is the propellant. This would be the longest hour of my life.

"Captain, ten minutes to the IP. We are on schedule, on altitude. We will be the third plane in the formation. Separation is 100 feet vertical and five seconds. Set the altimeter at 29.98 inches of mercury!"

The captain put his hand up and held the mike tightly to his throat. When he spoke, it was in a conciliatory voice. It was not the captain we had come to know.

"Gentlemen, I am not suggesting this course of action, but if our bombs do not automatically release and we counted to five and pickled them, we would dump all over the planes at Antung."

Of course he was suggesting it, and every member of the crew wanted to do exactly what the captain was suggesting. At that moment, our feelings for Smith changed.

"Now, gentlemen," the captain continued, "if we were to take this bizarre path, we'd first have to stuff an ample supply of cotton under the camera lens. We certainly don't want a record of actions tonight. The cotton will pass for clouds."

The gunners scurried to do as the captain suggested. Lieutenant Sharp had made his mind up. He would not drop by shoran tonight.

One minute to IP.

"Sharp, it's your plane. Have you selected a target?"

"I sure have, sir, but the bombardier is going to have to pickle the bombs."

"Roger on that," Captain Dudendorf said. "Finally I can get in the war. Rest assured there will be a lot of airplane parts flying around down there. I hope there is a pilot in every one of them."

"Bomb bay doors open," Sharp said. "I will give you a slow count, Bombardier.

"Five...four...three...two...one...pickle!"

Dudendorf had anticipated it perfectly. Every man at every station in the aircraft watched the ground below erupt in fire and smoke. Each of the eleven men screamed their approval and thanked the captain for making the suggestion.

Now it was time to get the hell out of there. We had expected to see a bunch of MiGs, but not a single plane came up to meet us. Not a puff of smoke, not a searchlight. Nothing. There must have been a hell of a party going on down there.

The flight back to South Korea was uneventful. As soon as we crossed the front lines, every man in the plane spoke on the intercom. Jokes were told, congratulations were given, and pride fattened the earphones.

"Crew, this is the captain. One thing you should know before we land. If anyone finds out what we did tonight, we may be put in front of a firing squad. What we have done is illegal as all get out, so laugh about it, talk to each other about it, but keep it in the plane."

"Gentlemen," I added, "I want to congratulate each and every one of you. We blew up a lot of planes tonight. Some revenge for all those 29 crews that never made it back. I'm damn proud of you guys."

774 touched down and taxied to its hard stand where a bus awaited. That had never happened before. We always had to wait a few minutes for the bus to come while we signed the log, shut down the aircraft, grabbed our chutes, flak jackets, duffle bags, and exited the aircraft.

"Captain," the bus driver said, "there is a meeting of all base personnel in the briefing room. Colonel Dornay has asked that I get you there as fast as I can. Something's up."

I knew what, and I could hardly swallow. We walked into the briefing room where every colonel, every light colonel, every major on the base awaited. I'd never seen so much brass in one place before.

The vision of Antung exploding twenty thousand feet below our aircraft repeated itself time and time again and, oh, how I wished we had followed orders and dropped on Sinuiju. Colonel Dornay walked to the center of the stage. He was not a happy man. The room quieted and he spoke in a stentorian voice.

"Okay, who did it? Who disobeyed my direct orders and bombed Antung last night? Which of you bastards got me a call this morning from the White House? Who's responsible for me getting my ass kicked by the Air Force Chief of Staff a half-hour ago? Which one of you guys made sure I will never have a star?

"Before you say anything, I should tell you that your actions last night countermanded a direct presidential order. That's right, an order we received directly from the president, and the penalty for disobeying a presidential order during war is death by firing squad. Let me repeat that. Whoever did this thing can be sentenced to death."

At that moment my sphincter was the size of a pea. Thank God for cotton!

The colonel continued. "I'm assuming the guilty party isn't totally stupid and probably put cotton beneath the camera lens to simulate clouds. That may or may not work. We will all wait here until the strike photos have been seen. If they produce nothing and no one has confessed, I will close the base until someone does. There will be no R & Rs, no visitors, no trips to the beach. We will fly practice missions every day we are not flying combat. The PX and the officers' club will be closed."

At that moment, I was sweating like a stuck pig and praying to God that our photos were blank. Just then an airman walked onstage carrying a large manila envelope, which he handed to Dornay. The colonel looked at the contents and turned to the audience. There were more than seven hundred airmen in the room and not a sound was heard.

"So you think you're so goddamn smart. Smart you are not. Stupid, yes. You never thought that turbulence might shake the cotton balls free of the lens, did you? Well, that's exactly what happened and I am looking at strike photos of Antung blowing sky high."

He paused. I was halfway through the "Our Father" when he called, "Captain Smith, Lieutenant Gushee, Captain Dudendorf, Lieutenant Sharp." The general named every officer on our crew. "Stand up!"

I wanted to be back in my T-6 running low on fuel and lost somewhere in Mississippi. I didn't want to be in a briefing room in Okinawa.

"Tell me, was it really worth getting shot for? Smith and Gushee, you are responsible for the actions of the crew while you are in the air. I could have you two before a court martial board before you could say Jack Robinson. I just don't know what you were thinking, and while I'm on the subject, if there is any other buffoon in the room thinks he can get away with defying our president, let this be a lesson."

Just as I was about to have a black bag placed over my head, I thought I heard a childish voice saying, "Tch, tch, you are naughty, naughty boys. Tch, tch!"

It wasn't a child's voice, it was our commanding officer and he was waggling a finger at us. "I am going to forget this little incident. Frankly I am damned glad you did it. But from now on, we all obey orders. Is that understood?"

No one who is being shot at likes to be told he can't shoot back.

Every man who flew in Korea supported General MacArthur and disagreed with President Truman when he fired the general because the general wanted to bomb Manchuria. On reflection, Truman was probably right, but then he wasn't in an airplane at twenty thousand feet being shot at.

I flew twenty-seven combat missions. I saw B-29s under attack by Russian jets. I watched the night sky fill with puffs of black smoke and felt the blast of antiaircraft shells lift my plane. I had engines on my 29 fail and engines hit by enemy fire, but I was never as frightened as I was at that moment standing in that briefing room listening to the colonel tell me that I was about to be put in front of a firing squad.

Chappy Goes to Press

The ubiquitous Chappy McDonnell. The laugh would suggest he has just pulled another prank.

I first met Chappy McDonnell in Greenville, Mississippi, and what a meeting that was! Chappy was Mr. Crazy and one hell of a pilot. He was also a talented entertainer. Chappy and I both played the piano and often entertained our fellow cadets at the Greenville Yacht Club, overlooking the Mississippi River. He was much better at it than I was. He wrote and produced a show at the base and we co-authored a song, which the cadets used to sing on their way to the flight line. It became the unofficial song of 52-Charlie.

After graduation from cadets, Chappy was trained in jets and sent to Korea to fly F-84s. He flew the F-84 like it was glued to his body and he thought combat was more fun than a toss in the hay. Chappy is the only pilot I ever met who volunteered to fly a combat mission in a T-6 over enemy territory while on a Rest and Recuperation leave rather than go to Tokyo for a hot bath and an evening of debauchery.

Chappy spent much of his time in Korea at the officers' club, making certain the whiskey was of the highest quality. He enjoyed it so much that when he retired from the service he bought a bar in Florida and entertained nightly.

I can't believe he ever made a nickel at CHAPPY'S, which was the name of his gin-porium. Anyone he met during his time in the service, and he met nearly everyone, was a non-paying guest. When I was there, Chappy even offered to close the bar so we could have it all to ourselves. He told me a wonderful story that night about a special mission he flew in Korea.

"Mole, I enjoyed my time in Korea. I flew 100 combat missions, dropped a bunch of bombs, torched a few enemy installations with napalm, and have a storehouse of memories that will last a lifetime. One of those memories was flying with Richard Hannah, a news reporter for *Flying* magazine, on a combat mission south of Pyongyang.

"Hannah was a super guy who really wanted to fly combat, so I made the arrangements. Our target was the North Korean tank and infantry school. Over 30 jets participated in that mission. The enemy must have thought it was the end of the world.

"You can't squeeze a reporter in the back seat of an F-84. It has no back seat. So, you know that T-33 that Quinn took you up in? Well that was our fighter that day and of course we didn't have any guns or ammunition. Hell, we didn't have so much as a water pistol. If we had encountered a MiG that day, the odds would have been heavily stacked in his favor."

Personally, I think Chappy would have found a way to destroy the MiG. He might even have talked him to death. He hadn't lost a bit of the guile that made me abort my third landing the day I soloed in Greenville.

"I had to twist Hannah's tail a bit before takeoff," Chappy continued. "You know, Mole, edge him up a bit?"

How well I knew.

"Anyhow, Mole, before taking off, I explained to Hannah how to bail out of the airplane. After all, we were going into combat and we might have been shot down. I took a long time explaining how to get rid of the seat, how to pull the D-ring of his chute and how to prepare to hit the ground … everything you have always wanted to know and were too scared to ask."

"You know, Chappy, it sounds just like you."

"Oh, one more thing, Mole, the night before our mission we played a little poker and I lost a few bucks to Hannah. As we were getting into our plane I said to him, 'I think I should pay you the money I owe you from the game last night in the event that we get shot down. I do like to settle my debts.'"

"That had an effect. Hannah spent the next hour working his beads and trying to make a few mental notes. The scratch pad he had attached to his knee bore no pencil marks when we landed.

"At one point in the flight, I turned the stick over to Hannah and suggested he might want to learn how to fly. We were being shot at by ground fire at the time. Hannah decided he didn't really want to be a pilot after all and asked me to resume control. We landed safely and Hannah wrote a fine article about the mission. He was a good guy and we had a bundle of laughs together."

McDonnell and Hannah met again many years later in southern California. Hannah had been hired as a press agent for Howard Hughes. Whenever he was contacted with a query about Mr. Hughes his response would be limited to, "No comment."

Chappy McDonnell got a law degree after he left the service. He resides in Florida, continues to play the piano and will entertain his friends whenever they are in town. He may be a few years older today than he was in Korea, but one would never know it.

Part pianist, part pilot, all crazy.

Back on the ground after the mission, Hannah is one happy reporter.

How to Piss off the Marines

Joe Guth in Korea. He flew several combat missions before being transferred to a highly secret group of select pilots.

I never met Joe Guth, but I was fortunate to meet his wife, Gilberta, who told me many stories about this exceptional pilot. Guth began his military career as a navigator on B-17s, flying submarine patrol out of Panama during the final months of WW II. When the war ended, he returned to college, completed his degree, and was recalled during the Korean War.

Guth had an itch. He wanted to be a pilot in the worst way. He was one of those few who was born to scream through the skies at Mach 1, twisting planes into contortions never anticipated by the designer.

Guth applied for pilot training and became a student officer in 52-Charlie at Greenville. He commanded a group of twelve student officers there, six of whom accompanied him to Williams AFB for single-engine jet training and subsequently went to Korea with him. Four of those six pilots were killed in action and a fifth, Bill Walker, suffered incurable brain damage due to anoxia. Jack Helms was killed when he flew his plane directly into the target. John Corbett was hit by flak on a dive-bombing mission and never bailed out. His plane exploded behind enemy lines. Al Rase ran out of fuel twenty-three miles offshore. His body was never found, nor was that of Billie Graham, who was shot down over enemy territory. Grady Hinson, Guth's best friend, was also killed in Korea.

Guth was posted to K-2 at Taegu but was transferred to a secret special weapons section at Komaki Air Base in Japan after flying only a dozen missions. He couldn't even tell his new wife what his mission was. It has since been declassified. Guth and his small group of combat pilots were flying F-84Gs equipped with atomic bombs, just eight short years after Hiroshima. Each pilot in his group was given a specific target in China, together with an escape and evasion plan should they be shot down. Guth knew that the odds were against a six-foot blond Aryan dressed in an American flying suit walking out of China.

During his flying career Guth had more than his share of problems, but Lady Luck was a constant passenger aboard his plane. Once, his maintenance crew connected the control cable to the elevator backwards. When he pushed the stick forward, the plane gained altitude. When he pulled it back, it dove. Not only did Joe manage to take the plane off, but he also flew it long enough to reduce fuel weight before landing successfully.

On another occasion, during a combat mission, he discovered that his fuel was being vented over the side. He barely made it to an emergency airfield where he landed with less than ten gallons of fuel, which was not enough to taxi his plane to a hard stand.

Some years later, his hydraulic system failed and he was forced to land without flaps. The runway was only 9000 feet, too short for a no-flap landing. The nose gear sheared off and the plane fell on its pylon tanks and caught fire. He blew the canopy and got out in the nick of time.

Guth's fondest memory came when he was selected to participate in an eighteen- month exchange program with the marines at Cherry Pointe, North Carolina, flying the F-9F8 Cougar jet and the F-4D Skyray.

It was a demanding assignment. The hours were long and the training intense. Nevertheless, he loved every minute of it. The final stage of the exchange program consisted of a Top Gun competition at Guantanamo Bay in Cuba. The rivalry was fierce and the last thing the Marines wanted was to have their competition won by a visitor. But that is exactly what happened. Guth won and at a parade held in his honor, a silver trophy was presented to him. The commanding general of Cherry Pointe was heard to whisper to a fellow marine, "I can't believe I'm handing this to an Air Force poag!" (Poag is a kind word for asshole or dipshit.)

Why couldn't the general believe an Air Force pilot would take their trophy? After all, Joe Guth was a member of 52-Charlie.

Guth died in 1998 from an illness caused by his 1953 exposure to nuclear radiation during his attendance at an atomic shot in the Nevada desert. The girl he fell in love with and married, Gilberta, wrote an excellent book about Joe entitled, *Fighter Pilot's Wife*. Gilberta recently married Guth's best friend and the best man at their wedding, Colonel Howard Pierson, an outstanding pilot and, of course, a member of 52-Charlie.

Color Blind

Roy Black dressed to kill in Korea.

Roy Black was raised in a small farming community in Lithia Springs, Georgia. He was Deep South all the way, with an accent you could cut with a knife. Seventy years later he is still in Georgia and his accent hasn't changed a bit.

Somewhere in those seventy years, Black saw the world and loved it. He came from moderate means and wanted to attend Michigan State University but couldn't afford it. He persisted, however, and earned a college degree in Georgia.

Black's ticket to the rest of the world was the United States Air Force. He applied for aviation cadets and was accepted. He completed his basic training at Columbus AFB and his advanced training in jets at Williams. He received his wings and after a stint at Luke, Black was given orders to report to K-2 in Taegu.

Black thought this was all fun and games. Each mission he flew was a walk in the park. He dropped his bombs; he fired his guns, and reported early for cocktails at the officers' club.

Shortly after Black arrived at K-2, Major John Whitehead was assigned to his squadron as the operations officer. He immediately named Black the assistant OPS officer. The major had flown in World War II. He had been a member of one of the most illustrious units to come out of that war. John Whitehead was a Tuskegee airman and he was the only black pilot at K-2. Little old southern boy, Roy Black, reported to John Whitehead, and while some might have thought there would be friction between the two men, there was none. In fact, the two pilots became fast friends.

Black addressed his friend not as Major or Sir, but as "Whitey," and John in turn called his new friend "Blackie." And it was always accompanied by a smile.

On April 13, 1953, the two men were scheduled to fly a four-plane formation against some marshalling yards near Wonsan, about seventy-five miles north of the DMZ (demilitarized zone).

Blackie carried two five-hundred-pound bombs, eight 4.5 rockets, and 1800 rounds of 50-caliber machine-gun bullets.

The other three pilots in the complement carried the same.

They dropped their bombs, fired their rockets, and shot every bullet they had at the train tracks. As they completed their low-level mission, every pilot in the group was hit by ground fire. John Whitehead was in serious trouble. His 84 caught fire. The fuselage, the cockpit, even the tail assembly were ablaze. Fire trailed 100 feet behind his plane.

Blackie screamed at his friend, "Whitey, get the hell out! Get out!"

But Whitey was too low. Every warning light in the cockpit flashed as the major twisted his aircraft trying to reach altitude. Whitey snap-rolled the plane and as he did, the fire blew out. The fire had been so hot that all the markings on the aircraft had burned off.

Blackie led the major to K-18, which was the nearest base.

"Mayday! Mayday! I need some help here," Blackie yelled.

The tower cleared the formation to land on runway 090. Whitey struggled to line his aircraft up and as he did, the tower changed the direction 180 degrees to runway 270. A completely new approach was required.

The major had no hydraulics; he couldn't get his gear down, nor his flaps, which meant he would have to belly his plane at an airspeed exceeding 200 mph on a very short runway. The prospect was not good.

Whitey lowered the plane's nose, aimed for the runway, and when he touched down, his plane caught fire once again. It flipped and headed backwards down the runway, flames spreading out in front of him. Parts of his aircraft littered the runway. Along the side of the runway were large mounds of sand. Whitey's plane plowed into one of the dunes and scattered sand as far as the eye could see. But fortunately the sand put out the fire. These were the same sand dunes that had claimed Reider's T-6.

Black landed with his wingmen. They all did their best to avoid the large chunks of Whitey's aircraft that were strewn along the runway. Black pulled off the runway and watched as Whitey opened the canopy of a plane that virtually had vaporized and climbed calmly down. The major was dazed but not hurt or burned.

The medical helicopter landed and the doctor brought his bag over to the four pilots. He opened it, pulled out a bottle of whiskey, and gave eight ounces to each pilot. All four F-84s were class 26; that is, they were destined for the scrap heap. America lost four aircraft that day, but Roy Black swears they blew the living hell out of a marshalling yard.

Blackie flew an additional twenty missions and when his tour was over, he resigned his commission and returned to Georgia where he entered the construction business. John Whitehead, who had been raised in Dublin, Georgia, less than a hundred miles from where Blackie was born, stayed in the Air Force as a career officer.

In the years that followed, Blackie would call his friend from time to time. I expect the conversation might have gone something like this:

"Hey, Whitey, what's up?"

"That you, Blackie?"

"You bet your black ass it is, Whitey!"

It's extraordinary how many wonderful friends you can make if you are colorblind.

Major John Whitehead graduated with the Tuskegee airmen. Better known as Whitey, and Blackie's best friend.

A Deadly Game Played in the Skies over Texas

Steve Sheedy before he met Duane Grobman. The two pilots destroyed more planes in America than they did in Korea.

The capacious skies pilots call home can be a warm and inviting paradise or a deadly dreamscape filled with cumulonimbus anvils and wing-shearing turbulence. Even a cloudless sky can be a terrifying playground when vigilance gives way to presumption. Duane Grobman and Steve Sheedy told me how they almost killed each other flying over Big Springs Texas. The two had earlier completed a combat tour in Korea with only about minor inconveniences, before surviving a mid-air collision at seventeen thousand feet on a clear day.

Sheedy began the story; "I went through basic at Greenville and advanced at Reese before completing my combat training in the F-51 at Luke. I was then posted to K-10 at Pusan in Korea along with several other members of 52-Charlie, including Duane Grobman, Pete Bolvig, Bill Hunter, and Mel Montie. K-10 didn't exactly welcome us with open arms. We'd been on the base for two weeks before command even talked to us and when they did, they said, 'We're phasing out the 51 and taking on the 86, so we don't want you here. We can't use you. Where would you like to go?'

"I offered to go home, but that was not an option. We opted for the 45th squadron at K-14. Orders were cut, and off we went from the southern-most base in South Korea to the northern-most. When we arrived, we were told we weren't wanted there either. They had all the 51 pilots they needed. Finally, after we'd been in Korea about a month, the 15th Recon Squadron agreed to take us on if we'd check out in the RF-80 and shoot pictures rather than guns during our 100 combat missions."

"Kodak moments, I declare! Did you ever fire a shot in anger?"

"Oh, yeah, there were a few times we carried rockets and 50 caliber ammunition."

"Any unusual missions?"

"Not really. With one exception, they were pretty routine."

"Tell me about the exception."

"I had just fired my rockets and was about to return to the base when my wingman and I decided to look around for a target of opportunity. We found one and as I dove on the target shooting my guns, those unfriendly people on the ground began shooting back.

Whack! I was hit and hit hard. The plane jumped like a spooked horse. I caught a 30 mm shell right below my feet in the nose of the aircraft. It destroyed my guns and left a sizable hole in the nose. That's all the prompting I needed. I beat a hasty retreat back to my base."

"That must have been pretty exciting!"

"It really was nothing, Ted. I'm embarrassed to tell you about it. There were so many members of our class whose missions were far more dangerous than that. Write their stories. They were the real heroes. They constantly returned to base with holes in their wings or their tails or their fuselage—if they returned at all."

"I know, Steve. But don't sell yourself short. A 30 mm shell exploding just below your feet isn't exactly a day at Disneyland."

"S'pose not."

"How about you, Duane? Anything to report?

"Yes, Sheedy and I followed each other around the world. We were, and are, good friends though for the life of me I don't under-

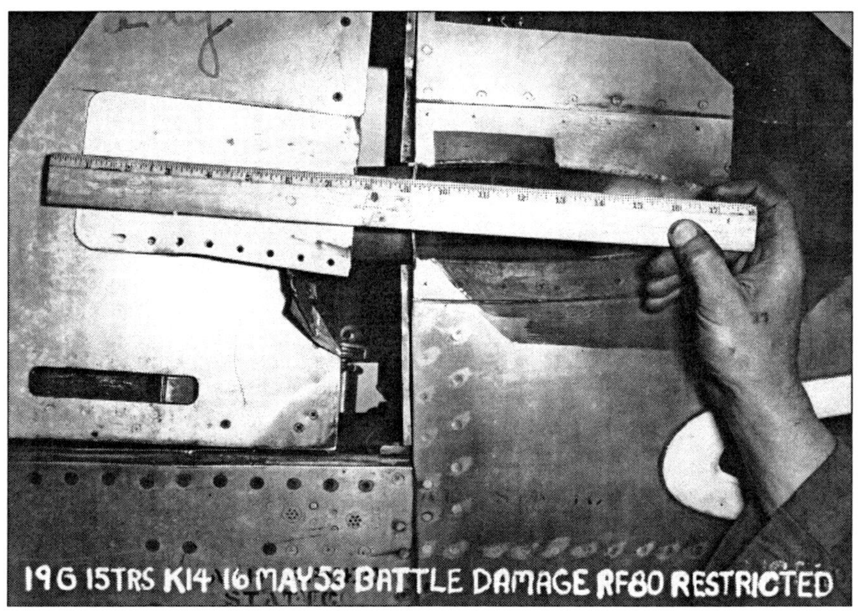

A 30 mm shell in the nose of your aircraft can ruin your day. Just ask Steve Sheedy.

stand why. Sheedy is a carrier. Virtually everywhere we went together something vexatious happened. While we were checking out 51s at Luke, Steve and I agreed to meet at a point over Yuma, Arizona. About the time he showed up, my engine quit and the silence roared. I couldn't restart it so I had to crash land the plane in Yuma. That was just the beginning.

"Next thing I know I am on my way with Steve to a base in Korea where we weren't wanted. We were told we couldn't fly the planes we could fly and had to fly the planes we couldn't fly."

"I understand you were awarded the Distinguished Flying Cross. Can you tell me how you got it?" I asked.

"I guess so. It happened at K-14 when I was flying RF-80s. We'd

Duane Grobman getting set to go on a photo shoot in his RF-80

received word that there was a downed pilot near the Yalu and they wanted some pictures to help locate the pilot for a pickup. I don't know how many passes I made or how many pictures I took. I was there a long time. There were four F-86s flying cover for me when a gaggle of MiG-15s appeared. Most 86 pilots would relish the opportunity to engage the enemy. For some reason, these guys decided to head home, leaving poor little old me all by myself.

"I continued to take pictures for several more minutes despite the fact I knew I had an audience. The MiGs hung around for a while before they decided they'd had enough of war and headed back to Antung. I guess the powers that be thought that was sufficient reason to hang a medal on me."

"The odds were not exactly on your side, were they, Duane."

"No, they weren't," he answered, "one F-80 against three MiGs. It would have been over quickly had they chosen to hang around. But they didn't."

"Did they ever find the downed pilot? "

"No, I'm sorry to say they never heard from him again. But if you're interested, I do have a story about another near disaster with Sheedy in Big Springs, Texas. This time he damn near killed me.

"I'm all ears."

"You remember, Ted, that one of the first things we were taught in cadets was to keep our heads on a swivel, that we live in a 360-degree world. Danger lurks, not just in front of our aircraft but also behind it, above it, below it, and on both sides. We were taught that accidents can happen on the roads we fly, as well as the roads we drive and often for the same damn reasons.

"Steve and I were instructor pilots at Webb AFB in Texas. My student was an Italian and Steve's was a Turk and their English left a lot to be desired. Time was short and if our students didn't complete all their requirements in one final day of training, they wouldn't graduate. But that would be impossible as the students had to fly in the back seat to get their instrument rating and the front seat to complete their combat requirements. Steve and I decided to stick them in the backseat, and fly their aerial maneuvers for them. A third pilot, I think his name was Baker, together with his student, joined us and off we went into the wild blue yonder.

"We had completed all our instrument requirements when Sheedy and I decided to simulate combat. Sheedy broke off and began to attack me. I took evasive action. I raised the nose of my T-33, flipped it over, pulled the stick back, and began a split S. In the meantime, Baker, who had no idea what the hell was going on, continued to fly straight and level. Now as I entered my dive, my whole life flashed in front of my eyes. Right below my plane was Baker. I couldn't avoid him. He was directly in my flight path. We hit amidst a monstrous crunch. I can still hear that awful sound. I sheared off his entire tail section, and, in the process lost my right wing.

"Two unflyable fighter aircraft were wobbling around at seventeen thousand feet on their way to the ground. Baker ejected first, followed by his student. My student was next and while I was the last to bail out, I was the first to land. A seat from the other aircraft lodged in the canopy of my chute, ripping apart some panels. It stayed in the canopy until I hit the ground. I made a fast but fortunately safe descent.

"In the meantime, Sheedy hit the debris field and tore off his pitot tube, which activates the airspeed indicator. Without that indicator, landing a plane is difficult and dangerous. Steve called the tower and asked a standby plane to take off and guide him in for his landing.

"Two planes were totaled. A third required major surgery, but all three pilots and their students survived without injury.

"An accident report was filed and the base commander ordered an investigation to determine if court martial proceedings were in order. The investigators ruled that the midair collision was an unavoidable accident, not pilot error, and Steve and I were acquitted.

"The incident was filed and forgotten, but not by Steve nor me. I learned something that day, Ted; I learned to live at least five zip codes away from Steve Sheedy."

Flying Formation with a MiG

I flew to targets throughout North Korea, with names you couldn't pronounce— TokTongNi, Taechon, SonJong, SaksanDong. Most of these missions were milk runs, but there were exceptions.

On May 18 I flew my twentieth combat mission against UnSan-Dong, a target with little strategic value. It was a mission that would remind us once again that our B-29s were old planes and our engines were tired engines. Every crew in the squadron had lost at least one engine due to mechanical failure. We had just dropped our bombs and turned for home when a MiG-15 sidled up to our right wing with his running lights and his cockpit lights on, begging to be shot at. The pilot wore a helmet but his face was visible and he stared at our cockpit.

Railton, flying central-fire-control (CFC), saw the MiG. "Request permission to shoot!"

"Negative on that!" I screamed into the throat mike. "You pull the trigger and I'll come back there and blow your head off!"

"But, sir, he's a sitting duck."

"And so are we, Private."

The MiG didn't have airborne radar. They couldn't see us at night. Their ground radar could pick up a 29 and guide a MiG towards that aircraft slowly until the MiG could see the flames from the 29's exhaust manifolds. In that position, the MiG couldn't fire on the 29 as his guns were aiming forward. What those crazy bastards did was have ground radar position a second MiG a half-mile behind the 29.

The MiG flying formation would turn on his lights. As soon as the gunners in the 29 opened fire, the second MiG would dive at the source of the tracers and fire its 37 mm cannon. We had lost a couple of planes that way and we never seemed to hit the goddamn MiG. We were there to drop bombs, not fight MiGs.

Smith turned sharply into the MiG and flew through the compass rose, (360 degrees) twice, while losing eight thousand feet. The MiG pilot never missed a beat. He followed us every inch of the way. Our radio operator called for help and a flight of F-94s arrived within minutes and chased the MiGs back to the Yalu.

No sooner had the 94s chased the MiGs away, than our number-four engine failed. We still had three turning, so we decided to make the trip home and skip going back to K-2. As we passed the tip of South Korea, a second engine called it quits. Now we were marginal. Our safety factor was feathered and we couldn't make it back to Kadena. We contacted Itazuke tower in Japan and they gave us a heading to the field.

About then we flew into a snowstorm. We couldn't see a thing. We turned on the deicers and prayed ice wouldn't build up on the leading edge of the wing. We had only two turning and those two engines wouldn't take an iced-up B-29 very far. It was comforting to know that someone was watching. Just then we lost radio contact. It was time to bring out the prayer beads.

Three minutes later, the radio crackled and we had contact once again.

"774, this is Itazuke tower. I forgot to tell you guys that we often lose communications with an aircraft during a heavy storm, and you are in a heavy storm. Should it happen again, continue on your last heading and altitude until we reestablish. I don't think we'll have any further problems. You're only a hundred miles from the base. By the way, the weather here is CAVU (ceiling and visibility unlimited). Our temperature is 83. You should be breaking into the clear in the next ten minutes."

Ah, the power of prayer!

Forty-five minutes later we landed at Itazuke and shut down. We were exhausted. Flying in a snowstorm, not knowing exactly where you are and having two engines feathered can take its toll. We remained in

Itazuke for two days before our new engines were mounted. In those two days we had an opportunity to visit Fukioko and the surrounding areas. The Japanese were very gracious hosts and there were many things to see and do. We went shopping, took in a hot bath, made some new friends, and opened a few bottles of scotch. Two days later we were back at Kadena planning our twenty-first combat mission.

Landing a B-29 When You Can't See the Nose of the Aircraft

My next mission was the most frightening of my entire combat tour. The trip to the target was uneventful. We experienced no flak or enemy interdiction. We arrived at the IP on time and the AP without incident. We dropped our bombs and learned later our circular error was under a hundred feet and were given a bottle of whiskey as a reward.

Mechanically the plane was sound. The engine purred. There was no turbulence. No storms—a sea of tranquility in the air and in the ocean.

We listened to armed forces radio and chatted freely amongst ourselves.

As we approached Okinawa air space, the first sour note of the night was broadcast by flight control.

"774, we have weather here. We are zero visibility. A GCA will be required. We have our very best operators on duty. The fog is so thick that after landing, each plane must come to a stop on the runway and wait to be guided back to their hard stand by a FOLLOW-ME jeep. It is going to take some time to recover all the 29s. We estimate that your landing will be in forty-five minutes. In the meantime go to the outer marker and remain at your present altitude until you are given further instructions."

Forty-five minutes! The pressure was back. We had been in the air ten hours and I was tired. We had at most an hour-and-a-half of fuel left. In any other part of the world, we would have been sent to an alternate field where the weather was more suitable for landing. But there is no other field near Okinawa. The only other place we could land was the ocean, and the runways there are wet.

Forty-five minutes passed, during which time we were instructed to let down from twenty thousand to fifteen hundred. Another ten minutes followed before it was our turn to land. We were guided into the pattern and had to repeat every instruction we received.

"774, take up a heading of 175 and hold your altitude at 1500 feet. Lower your flaps to 15 degrees. You are now on the downwind leg."

"Roger, flaps at 15. Turning to 175 at 1500."

"774 turn to heading 085 and slowly let down to 1000 feet. You are now on base leg. Flaps to 30 and lower your gear."

"Roger, turning to 085 at 1000 feet. Flaps at 30. Gear is down, three greens."

"774, in fifteen seconds I will turn you over to final control. After that you need not acknowledge any further transmissions. Do you understand?"

"Roger, understood."

"Good evening, 774. This is your final controller. Please turn to a heading of 355. You will be descending at the rate of 300 feet per minute. If you do not receive a transmission from me every five seconds, pour the coal to it and take it around. Normally, 774, if you do not see the runway when you break through 200 feet, we would ask you to take it around. Not tonight. It's zero here. But not to worry, we will bring you in.

"774 you are on the glide path and you are on your glide angle.

"774 you are ten feet below the glide path. Add power. You are on your heading. Your correction is excellent. You are on glide path, on heading. You have one minute to touchdown."

It was at this point that everything went to hell. In a high-pitched voice, Smith yelled at me, "Gushee, I want you to handle the throttles and the rudders. I will take the elevators and ailerons. When you see the ground, take over and land this thing."

Two people landing one airplane is like having two people drive a car, one on the brakes and one on the accelerator. But this was not the time to argue with the captain. I knew I would have to take all the surfaces away from the captain at some point and land the damn thing myself. The prospects were not good. We couldn't see a thing and coordinating surfaces with Smith was virtually impossible.

"774 you are a hundred feet below the glide path and wide right. Add power now and turn left to 350.

"Add more power, 774. You are now almost two hundred feet below glide path. If you don't correct soon, I will have to send you around."

I added the power without asking the captain.

"Nicely done, 774. You are back on the glide path. Return to 355 heading.

"774, you are on the glide path and heading. Everything looks great. You will begin to flare out in ten seconds. You should touch down in fifteen. When you see the runway, take over and land visually.

"On glide path. On heading. Looks great."

"Goddam it, Gushee, do you see anything?"

"No, Captain."

"Well, look, for Christ's sake. I don't want to crash!"

"774 begin your flare out. Touch down in five. This will be my final transmission. Good luck, 774."

"I see the ground, Captain. I've got the plane." I lied. I never saw the ground before we touched down, but I couldn't have both of us landing that plane. I took over, flared out, and within two seconds we touched down.

"Thank you, GCA, one hell of a job, I owe you a case of beer, and I will deliver it. We are waiting for the FOLLOW ME. By the way, we never saw the runway before we landed."

Smith was infuriated. "You lied, you bastard! You never saw the runway? You could have killed us all!"

"I thought I saw it, Captain, but what the hell, we made it and didn't blow a tire."

Fifty years later I can still see us in that cockpit. I can still see the darkness and feel the uncoordinated efforts of two pilots trying to land one plane. I can still smell the fear and hear the piercing voice of our airplane commander. I still remember the pride I had in landing without ever seeing a foot of runway.

Captain Smith flew only one more mission before he was removed from flying status and given a medical discharge. We had our differences, but Captain Smith was a fine pilot who truly cared for his crew. He flew combat during WW II when most bomber pilots were shot down by their twentieth mission. He was called away from his family five years after that war ended and asked to risk his life yet again in combat. He was tired and he was scared.

Our crew was assigned a new airplane commander, Captain Holmes. He was a superb pilot, a delightful and humorous man, and a joy with whom to fly. Every man on the crew liked Holmes. We even looked forward to flying combat with him. I had seven more combat missions, and they were all milk runs. We never saw flak or an enemy aircraft again. Our bombs were on target and we had a very happy crew.

Our new A/C, Captain Holmes, checks the flak-suit cart. Holmes replaced Captain Smith.

MiG Alley

Ed Izbicky and his favorite plane, the F–86. This is not the one he left in North Korea.

I met Ed Izbicky at Vance AFB where he had been transferred out of multi-engine aircraft into T-6s. Izbicky wanted to be a fighter pilot. Vance had a full complement of T-28 trainers, more powerful, more agile than the T-6, and an excellent plane from which to transition into jets. However, the T-28s were grounded because their props kept falling off. By the time Izbicky received his silver wings and gold bars, he was a good pilot but not a competent fighter pilot.

Precision flying is pivotal to a combat pilot but it must become reaction flying. If you have to think about the mechanics of a maneuver you're not looking for the enemy, or planning your attack or your evasion. You have to look up, down, front, back, left, and right and do it all at the same time.

A fighter pilot is as much a part of the aircraft as is the vertical stabilizer, or the wing flap, or a trim tab. Instinct guides a plane in inverted flight or whips it through a six- point slow roll.

Precision and reaction are musts for any pilot but especially a fighter jock.

After graduation, Izbicky was transferred to Wichita and upgraded into jets. He spent two-and-a-half weeks in the T-33, his hair on fire and his heart beating wildly and loving every moment of it. Next he checked out in the F-80 and learned the art of killing. He performed well. His reward: the F-86, America's hottest jet.

In January 2006, 52-Charlie held a reunion on a cruise ship to Alaska. Some fifty pilots and their wives attended. It was a wonderful moment to renew friendships and catch up on what had happened to those with whom we flew as cadets. Ed Izbicky and I sat in the lounge and ordered a couple of drinks, and he told me his story about combat in Korea, a story I will never forget.

"Gush, I had a hell of a time in Korea. I was stationed at K-14 Kimpo in the 4th fighter group. The day I arrived, there were dozens of B-29s sitting on the tarmac with shell holes in their fuselages, their engine nacelles, their tail surfaces, their cockpits. These 29s were scrap material. You poor son-of-a-bitch, you had to fly those things didn't you?"

"Yeah, but by the time I got to Korea they had switched over to night missions and after that only a few 29s were lost. My timing was pretty good. Enough about me, tell me about your experiences."

"I got to fly the F-86. I got to mix it up with the MiGs, and I was with the greatest group of guys I ever met. Most of them, Ted, were from 52-Charlie. Up to a point I absolutely loved it."

"Up to a point? Okay, you got my attention."

"Let me explain. My first mission was a milk run up to the front lines for a look- see. The next day the fun and games began. Our mission was high-altitude reconnaissance, to act as spotters for tactical aircraft like the F-84s, you know, that kind of stuff."

"Yeah, I know."

"We did not anticipate encountering any enemy aircraft that day, but of course we did. The MiGs weren't looking for a fight so they took off for Antung. The same thing happened the next two days; we encountered MiGs, and they hightailed it for home. No one else from my group ever ran into a MiG, so they started calling me 'Magnet-Hat, because I seemed to attract those bastards. Still, after twenty-five missions, I had never fired my guns in anger.

"I said I enjoyed flying combat up to a point, Ted. Well, the point came on my twenty-sixth mission, February 19, 1953. We were in our usual haunt, the Yalu River, and of course there were some MiGs around. I avoided them. But my wingman was flying his final mission and he wanted to get a MiG before rotating home. I agreed, and we broke into pairs and intercepted the enemy. The fight began. But even before I got a MiG in my sights, one of those bastards got on my tail and let loose with cannon shells.

"I heard a crunch. You have no idea what a horrible sound that was. A 37 mm cannon shell blew through the canopy behind my seat, right behind my goddamn head, just here," Ed said, pointing behind his ear. "Shrapnel shattered the seat and the partition between the seat and the headrest. I was hit in the shoulder and arm and blowing blood all over the cockpit. The shell blew the canopy off, along with my oxygen mask. The MiG strafed me a second time, hitting my engine compartment and severing the hydraulic lines. I lost control of the plane. It was on its way down.

"After twenty-six missions, my war was over. I bailed out at twenty thousand feet and waited until ten thousand to pull my ripcord. All in all, Ted, it was lousy day. When the chute opened, I got my second scare. The shell had torn six panels from the canopy. Fortunately the rags held together or I wouldn't be here talking to you."

"That's one thing I liked about the 29," I said. "I could have one engine shot out and still have three to play with."

"Well, if you call that flying, I suppose. Anyhow, I came down between two mountain ridges. I did my best to guide my chute to the edge of a wood but landed instead in a town named Yongsansi. Two members of the home guard took me into custody, did their best to treat my wounds. They gave me a bowl of seaweed soup and some rice. Later that night they blindfolded me, marched me down the road with my hands tied behind my back, and turned me over to the Chinese. Two of them knocked me down and kicked me. They took me to their air base at Mukden in Manchuria and threw me into a small rice cellar.

The next day a Chinese pilot who spoke no English greeted me. Using pictures and hand movements, he described how he had shot me down. He didn't miss a detail. The Chinese pilot smiled, bowed, and shook my hand. In the background were several men dressed in black flying suits. From their guarded conversation, I knew those bastards were Russian despite the fact the Kremlin maintained there were no Russians in Korean. Bullshit!

"Did the Ruskis talk to you?"

"Not a word. They kept in the background. The next morning they put me on a truck and drove me to Antung, where I spent the next few days."

"Christ, Ed, you were probably in Antung when I bombed it."

"That was you? You son-of-a-bitch. You damn near killed me. I remember the night. The air raid siren screamed. My guards took me from my cell and threw me into a hole outside. The ground shook, the earth flew into the moonlit night, and you know, Gushee, I laughed my ass off. When the raid was over, I was taken back to my cell. I couldn't figure it out, it didn't seem like a big raid, only one or two bombers."

"Only one, Ed, only one, and it almost cost me a trip to a firing squad."

"You're going to have to tell me that story when I finish. About then interrogation began in earnest. Eight to fourteen hours a day. I repeated my name, rank, serial number, and date of birth until I was saying it in my sleep. But I knew they'd insist on more, so I began to make up lies. I'm a pretty good liar, too."

"That doesn't surprise me."

"Still, I had to remember the lies because months later they would ask me the same questions and if my answers were different, there was hell to pay.

"Get this, Ted. My interrogator was a Chinese officer with long fingernails. He was as queer as a three-dollar bill and he was in love with Deanna Durban. He spoke English and played Durban's songs constantly, especially during interrogation.

"I told him that Deanna was a close personal friend and he damn near flipped."

"What were they trying to get out of you?"

"They wanted me to sign a statement saying I was guilty of germ warfare. They showed me pictures of 'bombs' with bugs crawling out. They weren't bombs; they were wing tanks that had been dropped during combat. Where they got the bugs God only knows. All I could do was laugh, which pissed them off. So I laughed all the louder. I called them slant-eyed bastards and told them to go screw themselves."

"You're kidding? Weren't you afraid they'd kill you?"

"Never entered my mind, besides, it kept me amused.

"One day I was moved to a farmhouse near the village of Uha-Dong where a young boy, a young girl, and an old lady were living. The young boy and the young girl disliked me and made it known, but I befriended the old lady. Each evening, a guard brought me seaweed soup, rice, and loaves of bread in separate containers. When the guard was distracted, I swiped extra loaves from the bread container and tossed them to the old lady. To show her appreciation, she would steal squash and cucumbers and corn from the fields and hide them in my sheets.

"The windows in the farmhouse were covered with rice paper so I couldn't see out. I kept poking holes in the rice paper, which pissed them off. They kept replacing the paper.

"Each day American POWs were marched down the street on their way to the Yalu River to work. As they passed my cell, they sang American songs. I poked some more holes in the rice paper and shouted my name. They yelled back, 'Take care! Resist! Don't let these bastards get you down.' And they'd laugh.

"Then I met the colonel! My new interrogator. This man was not to be dissuaded. He was going to get my name on the bottom of a confession one way or another.

"While interrogating, the colonel walked in a tight circle. Once, I fell in behind him unnoticed, walking the same circle. Suddenly the colonel turned about and damn near choked when he saw me. He told me that if I didn't sign the confession, he would sentence me to a hundred years of solitary confinement. I responded, 'Go screw yourself!'"

"You were out of your mind, Izbicky! I don't know why he didn't just shoot you and get it over with."

"I think he was a coward. Anyway, he only lasted about three weeks before a major replaced him. He was a real asshole. He had me taken outside where they forced me to dig a hole and stand in it while five Korean soldiers aimed their rifles at me. Orders were barked and triggers were pulled. 'Click! Click! Click! Click! Click!' There were no shells in the chambers. I was ordered to fill in the grave and was returned to my cell. This happened three more times.

"One day, I decided to sew an American flag. I pantomimed my wishes to the old lady and she provided me with a needle. I stole a pair of red basketball shorts from a clothesline and together with threads from the white bed sheet and my blue uniform I began to work in earnest. I completed the flag but destroyed it shortly thereafter as I was sure the young girl had seen it. A few weeks later, I began working on another flag, which I saved until I was repatriated.

"The war ended in July of 1953. For the first time since being shot down, I was housed with other American POWs. My old friend the colonel showed up one day and proudly denounced the sentences he'd imposed earlier. He did his best to befriend me and told me to go home, work on a farm and lead a peaceful life. A few days later, we were taken to an exchange area near Panmunjom where my picture was taken with General Underhall.

"That's it, Gush. It wasn't as bad as it could have been."

"Yeah, right." We finished our drinks and joined the ladies for dinner.

Ed Izbicky shows the flag he sewed while a POW to General Underhall on his repatriation. Picture is courtesy of the National Archives.

Izbicky stayed in the Air Force for twenty years—his life the service, his love the empty skies, and his heartbeat the throb of a jet engine. Fifty years after he was shot down in Korea, Izbicky typed in his name on Google and pressed the enter button. Several articles appeared on the screen, including one that left him speechless. It was an article that described in detail how Semen Alexeivich Fedorets shot down an American pilot whose name was Edward G. Izbicky. Fedorets was the same Russian pilot who downed American ace McConnell.

It took Izbicky fifty years to learn that he hadn't been shot him down on February 19, 1953, by a Chinese pilot, but by a Russian ace that wasn't even supposed to be in Korea.

The Mosquitos

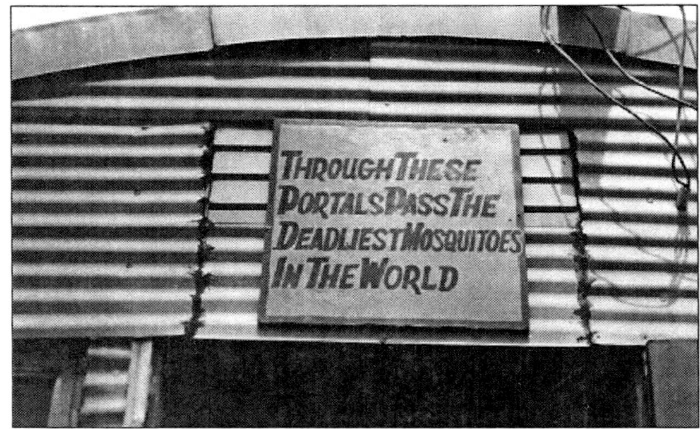

This sign hung proudly over the OPS room at K-47 in Korea, home of the Mosquito squadrons.

When the Korean War broke out, UN forces were having difficulty spotting enemy targets. Jeeps were used, but most roads near the front lines were impassable. F-51s and F-80s were impractical as the pilots were too busy avoiding enemy fire to accurately spot enemy formations. Observers were needed. Small training planes were tried, but they were too slow and too vulnerable. Someone in command proposed using the T-6 as a spotter aircraft. It was maneuverable and the pilot could concentrate on flying while the back seat spotter could locate and pinpoint targets of opportunity. But the T-6 was old and slow, and an easy target for ground fire. Command knew it would be dangerous but if it was effective, it might be worth the risk. It proved to be effective.

The Mosquito pilot would fly across the DMZ (demilitarized zone) to identify the target and determine the best way for the 80s or 84s to bomb it. Then, as the fighters watched from a safe distance, he'd dive on the target and mark it with a white phosphorus rocket called a "Willie Peter." What made these flights interesting was that during the ID of the target, the only enemy the North Koreans had to shoot at was one lonely T-6, so every enemy rifle, every antiaircraft gun, every rocket, every slingshot was aimed at this single T-6.

The fact that more T-6s weren't destroyed is a testament to the plane and its pilots. During the three years of the Korean War, the T-6 flew more than forty thousand sorties and demolished over 500 artillery pieces and1000 vehicles, killing an untold number of enemy soldiers.

Jim Kasparek during his training at Greenville where he first met the T-6. At the time he had no idea he would go to a jet war in a training plane.

Jim Kasparek took his T-6 experience beyond any measure of sanity. He went to war in the damn thing. Kasparek arrived in K-47 near the front lines in December of 1952, and before the war ended on July 27, 1953, flew more than fifty combat missions. His most memorable missions were his first and his last.

On his first mission he flew with Captain Homer Shinn, a check pilot, and were it not for him, Kasparek may have suffered the same fate as Quinn Fuller.

Their target was the infamous Old Baldy and Pork Chop hills. As Kasparek flew into the target, the ground became a maelstrom of twinkling lights. There were tracers coming up between his wing and the nacelle. They were so close he could hear them "crack" as they went by the canopy.

"I began evasive action as I was taught at Nellis, but Shinn yelled 'I have it!' He took over and bent the T-6 into configurations I had never seen before, configurations the T-6 was never designed to do.

"'Don't give the bastards a target,'" he explained. "'Keep this plane moving in every direction possible and all at the same time if you can. Forget that straight and level crap you learned at Nellis'."

Somehow Kasparek managed to escape the field of fire and complete his mission.

He learned you twist your aircraft into a pretzel if you have to. You do that or you die.

Captain Shinn saved his life that day and taught him how to fly combat in a reciprocal-engine aircraft. In the fifty missions that Kasparek flew he was constantly under fire but was never hit. He structurally weakened a whole bunch of T-6s, but he never returned with a hole in his wing.

When asked if he wore the heavy and cumbersome flak jacket into combat, Kasparek answered, "You bet I did. But not where you think. No one ever fired at me from above, only from the ground. I sat on my flak jacket. I was especially interested in protecting my future."

Kasparek's last mission was scheduled on the final day of the war. The cease-fire was to go into effect that night. Kasparek's squadron of eight aircraft under the call sign "Adverb" was told to observe the area but to stay south of the DMZ, in other words stay over friendly territory.

There wasn't any enemy action or ground fire that day, so Adverb 7 and one other member of Kasparek's flight made their own excitement by engaging in combat maneuvers. It turned tragic, however, when Adverb 7 snap-rolled at treetop level and dove into the ground.

Kasparek was contacted by his fight leader and asked to help locate Adverb 7. It didn't take long. Kasparek found the plane on the ground, smoldering with its wing wrapped over the canopy. There was no sign of life, which was confirmed by a ground recovery crew later that day.

What a waste.

Nye Shelton Spent Most of His Time in Korea Getting Shot At

Lieutenant Shelton stands in the one place in Korea where he wasn't being shot at, his base.

A T-6 hasn't much of a chance against the F-86. The T-6 is slow, the F-86 is fast. So when a friendly F-86 starts shooting at you, it is time for the worry beads. Lieutenant Shelton, 52-Charlie, may have the distinction of being the only Mosquito pilot who came under attack by an American F-86. War is tough enough when you have only the enemy to contend with. But when your own side starts shooting at you, it's time to take up another profession. On the day in question, Shelton was guiding a flight of four F-86s to a target when he heard over his command set that an 86 was on fire.

Suddenly, tracers arched their way past his canopy and his engine cowling and under the belly of his aircraft. Someone was shooting at him. He looked to the left and slightly behind and saw an 86 with fire coming from the left side of its fuselage. It was burning brightly in a tight spiral, spewing tracers from its guns. Those bullets were coming perilously close to his cockpit. Shelton noticed one other thing: the 86's canopy had been blown and the cockpit was empty. He was under attack by a phantom aircraft whose guns were being fired by an electrical system gone berserk. Shelton made a climbing turn to escape the jet and watched as it spiraled lazily downward and nosed into the earth. A huge fireball shot upwards.

Nye Shelton also found a way to be fired on by ground troops. The standard procedure for a T-6 spotter pilot was to fly his first twenty missions in the front seat of a T-6 with a combat instructor pilot in the rear seat. During this orientation period he learned the topogra-

Shelton at the front lines with Lieutenant Barng, his Korean liaison from the 9th ROK Division. Notice the helmet and the sand bags. This is heavy-duty stuff.

phy and boundaries of the area he would fly, as well as the procedures for locating and marking a target.

Once Shelton completed his first twenty missions, he was posted to an Army unit at the front line as a Forward Air Controller, where he could not only see the enemy but also watch as they shot at him. After three months on the front line, Shelton returned to his base to finish his combat tour flying the T-6 spotter. Nye Shelton flew fifty missions before the war ended and he was returned to the U.S.

One of his last missions was in support of a United Nations battalion that had come under heavy fire by a superior enemy force at hill 406, a strategically important hill that was in danger of being overrun. The war was nearing an end and the North Koreans were making every effort to gain as much ground as possible on the premise that what they possessed when the armistice was declared would belong to them.

The ground commander called for support. Shelton and his observer took over and coordinated the strike with a flight of 84s. He knew the area well. There was a river that formed a "dog's head" several miles from hill 406. He asked the 84s to follow the river from the dog's head to the point where it split and flowed around both sides of the hill. Each fighter carried two napalm bombs. Shelton directed the attack so that the napalm bombs overlapped. The enemy withdrew and never contested hill 406 again. It was estimated that 175 of the enemy were killed in that one strike.

Shelton was awarded the Distinguished Flying Cross for that mission, along with the personal thanks of a battalion commander whose group was under enemy fire.

Shelton's T-6 was hit on several occasions. He often landed with holes in his wings, or holes in the stabilizer, holes almost everywhere except in the cockpit, for which he was genuinely thankful. When his tour of duty was over, Nye Shelton returned to the States convinced that damn near everybody and everything in North Korea was shooting at him.

Coming in on Half a Wing and a Prayer

Mosquito pilot Ray Rottas wasn't supposed to fly T-6s. He trained in B-25s and upon graduation from cadets was sent to Randolph AFB to be checked out in a B-29.

He absolutely hated the 29.

"It's like sitting on your front porch and flying your house. I hated it," he said. "I had to get out. I told Command that I would volunteer to fly in Korea if they would let me fly anything but a 29."

Goodbye 29, hello T-6. Rottas joined the Mosquito pilots at K-47 and flew spotter missions for the next year. Like most of the pilots in his squadron, Rottas had his share of "memorable missions."

Particularly his 55th, when he was flying a close support mission along the front lines. He had three rocket markers under each wing. On that flight his back-seat partner was a jet pilot who wanted to see what it was like to fly combat in a T-6.

Rottas was flying over the target at 7000 feet when all hell broke loose. A 20 mm shell hit the rocket pack under his right wing and blew a hole in the wing large enough for a man to climb through.

Rottas told the pilot in the back, "Don't touch a thing back there. Keep your hands off the stick and your feet off the rudders. This plane is so out of trim it won't take much to put it in the ground." He was not trying to scare his passenger, but he knew the odds of landing the plane were slim.

"Would you like to bail out?" Rottas asked his passenger.

"Are you going to?"

"No!"

"Then I'm going to stick with it."

"Your option."

It was almost impossible to fly that T-6. One pod of rockets was dangling loose. Rottas could not maintain altitude. He had to severely crab right in order to fly straight. Once more he asked his passenger if he wished to bail out. Once again, the answer was, "No."

Rottas contacted the tower and declared an emergency. He was instructed to bail out. He refused. It would have been impossible to do so because the minute he let go of the stick, the plane would have snap-rolled and nosed straight into the ground. He couldn't get out of the crippled plane even if he wanted to.

The tower called again and ordered him to bail. Again he refused and told the tower to clear the runway, he was coming in. Then he switched off the command set. He didn't want to hear anything further from base.

The runway at K-47 lay between a mountain and an elevated railroad spur, some twenty feet in the air. Rottas knew he was too low to fly over the railroad, so he set a course to just miss the spur and the mountain. Ray had one chance at the runway. There would be no taking this T-6 around and he didn't know whether the flaps would work or whether the gear would lower.

He decided that if he got three greens, he would land on the runway. If he didn't, he'd belly it in on the grass next to the runway and hope for the best.

He was also concerned about the rockets dangling below his wing. Would they release when he touched down and if so, would they blow up?

Rottas had a lot on his mind. Just before touchdown, he had to kick it out of the crab he was flying and align it along the runway. As often happens in moments of great stress, he made one of his best-ever landings. He taxied the plane back to the hard stand where a very grateful jet pilot got out from the back, shook his hand, and swore he would never volunteer for anything the rest of his life.

Rottas lived on the edge of excitement. A few missions later he was the recipient of a 20 mm shell while cruising over enemy territory at about 7000 feet.

His engine quit. Things get very silent at a moment like this. His observer suggested he restart the engine, which may have been the stupidest suggestion ever made.

Rottas smelled gas. He knew he wasn't out of fuel, but he had little time to figure out what the trouble was. He grabbed the wobble pump and pumped as if his life depended on it, which it did.

He was now at 1500 feet and descending.

If the engine didn't catch in the next few seconds he would have to bail out over enemy territory, which meant he would become a POW.

Sput-sput-sput—the prop turned slowly. Sput-sput-sput—the engine caught.

"Climb, for God's sake!" was the next piece of advice from the rear seat. "Climb!"

Rottas chose not to. His air speed was just above stalling. He knew if he began to climb at that speed he would be an easy target for ground fire. So he firewalled it and snaked his way through the passes in the mountains back to the base. Lady Luck had a passenger for the second time in a month. But Rottas didn't want to test her resolve any further.

The reason Rottas' engine quit? Faulty spark plugs! Strange considering the crew chief had just changed the plugs on the plane. However, due to supply shortages maintenance was forced to use rebuilt plugs, not new ones.

A few weeks later Rottas was flying a front-line mission spotting for a group of F-86s. A plane had been shot down, and he was trying to locate it.

He went in at about 6000 feet with F-86s flying well above him. Again all hell broke loose. He was in a flak trap, being fired on by a radar-controlled gun. He twisted that T-6 every conceivable way, but it was useless. Unless he could quiet that gun he was going to be shot down.

Rottas called in the 86s and asked them to approach the gun from the rear. This they did and they blew it to hell.

Rottas reported his sighting of the radar-controlled gun in debriefing. But no one would believe him. The North Koreans did not have that kind of equipment, he was told. This had all the signs of a political denial. Someone somewhere didn't want the Chinese to have such an advanced weapon. So, when in doubt, turn your back.

This must have inspired Ray Rottas. After he was discharged he went into politics. He served ten years as an Arizona state senator with Sandra Day O'Connor and eight years as state treasurer.

If you can't beat 'em, join 'em.

White-Collar Job

Colonel Bob Hartwig claims he fought a white-collar war.
His plane was sabotaged. He crashed. His son was threatened by terrorists.
White collar, indeed!

Some people were born with chevrons on their arms. Such was Bob Hartwig. He was destined for the military. He was officer material and command was part of his personality. He was single-engine all the way—completed his training in F-86s at Wichita and Nellis and then was posted to K-14 in Korea.

Hartwig likened his experiences to a white-collar job.

"Fly up to the Yalu River in a high-altitude support mission, fool around a while, and then return to base."

When pressed, Hartwig admitted he often saw MiGs that dove down on his group shooting their 37 mm cannons until they exhausted their ammunition, at which time they turned tail for Manchuria.

Hartwig also admitted he'd engaged the enemy and was credited with one probable and a couple of MiGs damaged. Following one of these engagements, Hartwig was told his plane had been hit. There was a hole the size of a tennis ball on the top of his wing and an exit hole the size of a basketball on the bottom. The wing of an 86 is loaded with fuel and control cables, but the 37 mm shell that hit his plane missed the cables and didn't ignite the fuel. White collar, indeed!

The normal tour of duty for a fighter pilot in Korea is 100 combat missions. Hartwig flew 93, but that 93rd mission was his defining moment in Asia. Hartwig's plane had just returned from a major overhaul in Japan, where it had been either sabotaged or a careless airman had completed the maintenance. The likelihood, though not proven, was sabotage. Someone had left or placed and extra hydraulic bracket in his elevators. Hartwig flew an uneventful mission to the Yalu that day, but on landing at K-14 the bracket jammed the elevators as he touched down, causing the nose to shoot up. The plane soared fifty feet into the air, then stalled and crashed into the runway, knocking Hartwig unconscious. Hartwig's 86 caught on fire, but ground personnel were able to get him out before it blew up. Hartwig broke his ribs, his back, and his ankle and spent the next two months in hospital, most of it in a body cast. Eight months would pass before he would return to flying status.

Still, Hartwig was luckier than some of his friends, who lost their lives in Korea. One was a roommate who tried to roll his plane on takeoff and was killed when the plane crashed.

Bob Hartwig returned to the States, where his career took hold. He spent time in Vietnam in the 5th Air Force and was assigned as the USAF defense attaché to Turkey— where he got his greatest scare. A friend and his son were leaving the base on a back road together with Hartwig's 10-year-old son, when three terrorists in masks jumped up from a culvert brandishing machine guns and stopped the car. The terrorists were after Americans, but not kids, and when they saw the two young boys in the car they weren't sure what to do. Hartwig's friend quickly took off his watch and that of Hartwig's son and gave them to the terrorists, along with his wallet. That appeased the gunmen and they let the car go on.

The prime minister of Turkey called Hartwig to apologize for his countrymen. A year later, the watch was returned to him along with a note that several terrorists were killed in a shoot-out and one was wearing his son's watch. The watch no longer worked.

Hartwig ended his military career as a bird colonel commanding Maxwell AFB, the site of the War College. In 1979, after 28 years of service, he retired to civilian life and began "another" white-collar job.

A Half-Mile from a Career in the Air Force

Harley Lake on his way to war in a picture that has seen better days.

Harley Lake graduated from cadets at Reese AFB in Texas, having trained in the T-6 for twelve months. He went to Mooney for jet training in T-33s and F-80s and after a few weeks of gunnery school, it was on to K-14 in Kimpo, Korea, where he flew 100 combat missions in the F-80 and the F-86.

If you listen to Harley tell the story, these were simple, almost boring missions with hardly anything to stir the imagination.

"I spent most of my time mapping North Korean sectors, checking along the Yalu to discover enemy buildups of men and materials, taking a lot of pictures and spotting for attack aircraft.

"On occasion I would come under attack by ground fire. I watched the black puffs from the enemy's radar-controlled antiaircraft guns pop just behind my tailpipe, working their way towards me. Then it was time to change altitude and it would start all over again. Quite a game, I rather enjoyed it.

"Oh, I found a few holes in the fuselage or wings after a mission. Nothing dramatic. A couple of times, while flying the F-80, I was chased by MiGs, but when that happened, our 86s would tell me to go home and then they would engage the enemy. I had a feeling they were using me as bait."

Harley spent a lot of time over Pyongyang, one of the most heavily fortified positions in North Korea, bombing the airfield and outbuildings and taking an untold number of pictures. He was awarded the Distinguished Flying Cross for his activities in Korea.

When Harley returned to the States, he was sent to Dover, Delaware, to transport F-84s, F-86s, and L-20s to various bases around the country.

"I also spent time in Labrador and Greenland flying point-of-no-return flights.

These were especially challenging flights. If your navigation was faulty or you suffered mechanical failure, the chances of surviving the mission were slim. We simply didn't have the fuel to return to our point of origin. Several pilots were lost during these exercises."

Harley planned to be a career pilot. He enjoyed flying and he loved challenges. However, one day all this changed. Harley was fly-

The airstrip at Pyongyang. Count the bomb craters. Today a couple of guided missiles would do the job and do it better.

ing an F-84 over Paducah, Kentucky, when his engine began to fail. He could pull only about eighty percent power where ninety percent is required to keep you afloat.

Harley turned his aircraft immediately toward Fort Campbell,

Kentucky, an Army base, and declared an emergency. As he turned onto final approach, his engine quit. He couldn't lower the gear or the flaps, and the worst part was he was a half-mile short of the runway. There was a small grove of trees directly in front of his plane, which he could not avoid. Harley guided his 84 into the trees so that the branches would hit his wing root and not his canopy. He was successful and once he cleared the trees, he belly landed the crippled 84 safely in an open field, but in the process, he broke his back.

Some of the branches Harley sheared from the tree.

Harley's F-84. Note the rupture in the wing root where he hit the tree limb. The plane was totally destroyed.

Harley was taken out of his plane and spent the next full year in a hospital, where he was told his chances of walking again were slim. Harley never accepted that diagnosis. After a year, he walked out of the hospital to begin the rest of his life as a civilian.

Harley Lake and Bob Hartwig have a lot in common. Both crashed on landing, both broke their backs, both spent months in a hospital. Both walked out of their hospitals. Both continued to fly, Hartwig in the military and Lake in civilian life. Both look back on their time in the military, their time in the sky as the defining moments of their lives. Harley's only advice, "Avoid landing at an Army base."

Napalm, A-Bombs, Flak, and a Few Too Many Colonels

Don Burrell gets set to fly a colonel's wing, much to his chagrin.

Don Burrell completed his pilot training at Luke AFB in the F-84 before being sent to the 9th fighter-bomber squadron at K-2. There his flight leader was Lieutenant Tom Titus, an extraordinary pilot who was a bit on the wild side. One day Titus was forced to abort takeoff because of a fire in the cockpit. Titus pulled off the runway, jumped out of his plane, and ran as fast he could. The plane burned to the ground.

On another mission, Titus was forced to bail out over enemy territory. When he hit the ground, three Koreans ran after him. Titus reached for his .45, but it hung up in his flight suit—fortunately! The Koreans grabbed his hand and while shaking it, thanked him profusely for helping to save their country.

When you were scheduled to fly with a pilot who burned up one aircraft and bailed out of another, you were in for your share of excitement. Burrell flew with Titus on one of his first bombing missions and watched tracers shoot by his canopy and across the nose of his F-80. Burrell was lucky; none of the shells hit him, but the enemy did blow a hole about a foot in diameter just below the cockpit of Titus' 84. Titus had fuel on the cockpit floor and his radio was out, but he was still flying. He couldn't make it back to Taegu, so the two men

Titus points to the hole in his 84 caused by a MiG.

landed safely at K-13. There Titus commandeered Burrell's 84 and flew it back to K-2. Burrell had to grab a ride on the mail plane.

Burrell's choice of flying partners left something to be desired. Titus, though an excellent pilot, created nightmares for those who flew with him. Burrell next flew with his wing commander, a colonel, who was just a click crazier than Titus. The colonel led Burrell through the clouds into a valley to attack an enemy concentration. They were being fired on from both sides of the valley. When they returned to base, the colonel's rudder looked like Swiss cheese. Burrell's aircraft had also been ventilated. Following his tour in Korea, the colonel rotated back to the States and was arrested in Las Vegas for robbing hotel suites dressed in a cape and mask. He must have thought he was an airborne Zorro.

After K-2, Burrell went to Komaki, Japan, with Joe Guth, where he flew an F-84 with a Mark-8 atomic bomb. In the event of war, Burrell would fly to a target in Russia. He had sufficient fuel to get to the target and about halfway home before running out.

About now, Burrell met his second colonel, his new wing commander at Komaki. This colonel did everything by the book, and the book said that the recommended approach speed of an 84 for landing should not be exceeded. The colonel sat at the end of the runway, watching each 84 pilot land, and then gave them hell for exceeding the recommended approach speed. His men told him that if they brought their planes in at the recommended speed they would bust their asses. The colonel demurred. He assembled his men at the flight line and ordered them to watch him land his 84 at the recommended speed. But it wasn't the colonel's day. He stalled a quarter-mile short of the runway, destroyed his airplane and broke his back.

One thing Komaki had was plenty of colonels. Burrell's OPS officer, Col. Jack Lincoln, constantly reminded his group that they all had instrument cards and therefore could fly in all weather conditions. One day it was zero/zero and raining cats and dogs. The pilots suggested they wait for it to clear a bit before taking off. The colonel would have none of that. He checked out a plane and took off. The weather didn't improve and when the colonel returned, he landed with too much speed. Burrell and his friends drove to the end of the runway where they photographed the colonel's plane sliding into a canal. The colonel wasn't hurt, just a bit embarrassed.

Don Burrell had many exciting experiences in the Air Force. He flew napalm runs at such a low altitude he could see the faces of the frightened people trying to outrun the bomb. He flew with an A-bomb under his wing. He put a thousand-pound bomb in the front door of an enemy's ammunition dump and blew up much of the surrounding countryside. He attacked an enemy artillery position through a hail of ground fire that hit everything in the area except Burrell's plane. He flew with Tom Titus who spent an inordinate amount of time trying to get out of damaged aircraft.

And he got to know three colonels briefly and a fourth colonel very well. He married that colonel's daughter.

Rank Has Its Privileges

Flying in the number-two spot behind an aggressive leader can be very dangerous, as Chuck Levinger was soon to learn.

Recently Chuck Levinger, Warren Hunt, and I had lunch and talked about our Korean experiences. Levinger and Hunt did most of the talking and I did most of the listening. Levinger began:

"After graduation from cadets I checked out in the F-84 and was posted to K-8 in Korea, where I flew seventy-seven combat missions. I had a few close ones during that time."

"The floor is yours, Chuck. Tell me about them."

"On one of my first missions, our target was a North Korean marshalling yard, supplying materials to the front lines. I flew number two on the commander's wing and saw more flak over that marshalling yard than I would encounter during the rest of my combat tour. I learned something that day, Ted. I learned it's best to fly lead. Everything the North Koreans fired at the colonel's multi-striped aircraft missed. But much of it found another target. I heard a loud explosion and my 20-ton jet flipped over on its back like a leaf in the wind. Another shell exploded so close to the cockpit that I could smell gunpowder through my oxygen mask. Believe me, I could smell cordite."

"What did you do?"

Levinger checks out the ordnance Was this the one he would drop on the marshalling yard?

"My first impulse was to eject, but all my instruments appeared to be normal and I still had control. I released my bomb and, frankly, I didn't give a damn whether it hit the target. I would have settled for hitting North Korea. I contacted the colonel, told him I was hit and asked him to slow down because I couldn't keep up. The bastard wasn't about to slow down. He hightailed it out of there. The other two pilots in our flight were not in such a hurry. They pulled alongside and checked out my 84. They confirmed that there was a large hole in my fuselage behind the cockpit and many smaller holes in the tail section. But they also told me that my plane appeared to be stable."

"That was good news."

"True, but the bad news wasn't far behind. My base was below weather minimums, so I was diverted to K-2 along with every other 84 flying that day. Forty-eight of us! Forty-eight fuel-starved F-84s would have to land on a single runway in a damn short period of time.

"I was lucky. My plane was barely flyable so I flew a straight-in approach and had a ringside seat to watch as the other forty-seven came in. Do you remember Lindsay Bartholomew?"

"No, Chuck, I never met him. He didn't go to Greenville or Vance. Why?"

"Lindsay, one of my best friends, flew with me that day. As he approached the field for landing, he ran out of fuel, his engine quit, and he flamed out. Lindsay called the tower and told them he could dead-stick his 84 to a safe landing. They cleared the pattern for him, but there was a problem, Lindsay had never landed at K-2 before and didn't know that a trench lay just before the runway. Lindsay bellied it in, hit the trench, and exploded into a ball of flame. Ted, he never had a chance."

"I'm sorry, Chuck."

"That's war. Two other planes flamed out from fuel starvation but managed to land safely. My plane was a class 26; they salvaged parts and tossed the rest away."

"Well, I hope your luck improved."

"Actually, it didn't, Ted. I was asked to test fly an F-84, which had suffered battle damage and had just been repaired. Everything went along smoothly until suddenly the canopy blew open. The wind blew through the cockpit at 150-plus miles per hour. My eyes welled with tears. I could barely see but fortunately I managed to put it down and walk away. I've never been so cold in my life."

"What's your fondest memory of Korea, Chuck? Do you have one?"

"I guess so. A bittersweet memory. One day while standing down, I heard that one of our pilots was missing so I volunteered to fly a search mission. Fifth Air Force guided me to the area where he was last seen. I dropped down to the deck and circled, hoping to receive a radio contact from him. Nothing. I continued to circle the area until I was ordered to return to the base. The most frustrating thing for a pilot is to have to break off a search."

"What about the pilot?"

"He was never found. I flew back by way of the coastline. There were several small North Korean fishing boats and one very large sampan sailing in the ocean. We were forbidden to attack fishing boats but damn it, Ted, that sampan just didn't seem to belong amongst those fishing boats. I dropped down to three hundred feet and made a flyby. As I approached, the sampan opened fire and tracers spewed past my aircraft. I fired all six of my guns and walked tracers right into the side of the boat. The sampan was carrying munitions and disintegrated in one very large explosion, which almost took my plane with it.

"I got revenge for one of ours. Small consolation but it's a memory I will long cherish.

"There's one more vignette if you're interested."

"You bet. Talk on."

"I boast about this often. After Korea I went to Luke AFB as an instructor in combat training, which by the way was the precursor of the Top Gun program. There I met the senator from Arizona, Barry Goldwater, a brigadier general in the Air Force reserve. The senator wanted to be included in a flight so he could observe the training process and I was to be his pilot. Just before takeoff, Goldwater learned it was to be a high-altitude mission, which would play hell with his sinuses so he opted out. Military flying is a young man's sport. The senator made a wise decision."

"I can't blame you for boasting about meeting Goldwater. He was a fine man and an excellent governor."

And now it was Warren Hunt's turn.

The Man Who Invented Underwater Flying

Warren Hunt and his RO, Ray Harmiling, prepare for their final mission in Korea. Warren says he is the handsome one. Are we missing something?

"Okay, Warren, how about you? Got some Korea stories?" I asked.

"You bet I do. Did anyone ever tell you how I flew underwater?"

"No, but this one I have to hear."

"After I received my wings I checked out in the F-80 and then the F-94, the all-weather jet fighter that had airborne radar."

"I know the 94; it was the Christmas wish of all the B-29 pilots, me included. When you guys were in the area we were flying, the MiGs went home and all we had to face was ground fire. I think I had a love affair with the 94."

"You probably don't know this, but prior to entering cadets I flew as a crop duster."

"That explains it. Another one of the crazies."

"I looked forward to combat. They sent me to the 319th Fighter Interceptor Squadron at K-13, where I spent most of my combat tour supporting you guys in the 29s at night. As far as I know, not a single 29 was shot down by a MiG after the 94s became operational."

"You weren't at Sinanju during the run on the bridges. The MiGs were there, and I believe they got a 29 that night."

"Maybe. Maybe flak got him. Anyway you're interrupting my story. We didn't fly much during the day except to train and that got kind of boring at times. One afternoon three of us were flying around Inchon Bay where an American ship was anchored. I assumed its sailors were equally bored so I proposed we add a little excitement to their lives?

"I have a feeling the crop duster is about to take over."

"You're right. I told my two wingmen to stack high and follow me. I flew out to sea and then turned toward the ship. I intended to fly at water level and at the last moment, pull up over the ship. I instructed #2 to pass in front of the bow and #3 to pass the ship behind the stern.

"We pushed our throttles forward and I dipped to wave-top level. Just before reaching the ship, I noticed water rippling a few feet in front of the nose of my 94. Suddenly water covered my entire canopy. My wings were partly under water, only the vertical stabilizer was dry.

My RPM surged to 104 percent. That's not good. You reciprocal guys probably don't know that when water is injected into a jet engine it can mess it up something awful."

"I don't understand, Warren. Where'd the water come from?"

"The ocean, of course. I was flying so low and so fast that a vacuum was created under my wings, which sucked the ocean water up and over my aircraft.

"My #2 reported he was certain I had bought the farm. He saw a thin sheet of water engulf my aircraft. I was flying in a water bubble, proving once again nothing is impossible. I admit that only one in a thousand would have survived that experience. I learned a lesson that day that I will never forget.

Warren Hunt took the F-94 for a swim in Korea.

"I learned a second lesson a few days later. Never fly with a head cold. I was on patrol over my favorite river, the Yalu, waiting to be relieved by a Marine pilot. By the time he arrived, I was dangerously low on fuel, which meant I'd have to stay at altitude until I reached the base, as a jet's fuel consumption is much higher at lower altitudes. Once I reached the base, I'd have to make a rapid descent to land, which wouldn't allow sufficient time for the pressure inside my ears and sinus cavity to equalize. I had a head cold that day and that descent would damn near kill me.

"When I passed through 10,000 feet, I felt like a railroad spike was being driven between my eyes with a sledgehammer. I told the tower to have the flight surgeon meet me at debriefing. By the time

I landed I was bleeding from my nose and left ear. My eardrum had burst and the pain was the worst I ever experienced. I was grounded for ten days and chewed out by every superior officer on the base. Their message: You don't ever—*ever* being the key word—fly with a head cold. I'll tell you one thing, Ted, flying under water could kill you, but flying with a head cold is worse."

"You burst an eardrum, and they kept you on flight status? You're one lucky pilot."

"You're right about that, Ted. I am lucky. Once I spent five days in Tokyo with three of my flying partners on an R & R, enjoying the Ginza, the hot baths, and the low prices. The day we were scheduled to return to Korea, a friend, Lt. Jim Fitzgerald, asked if he could take my place on the C-124. His wife was expecting and he was anxious to get to her. The four of us decided to toss a coin to see who would stay in Tokyo and who would return with Fitzgerald on the 124. I won and got two more days in Tokyo.

"Fitzgerald and my three friends boarded the 124 that rainy evening, and on takeoff the C-124 lost both engines on the port side. The plane flipped over and killed all 120 passengers and crew."

"First Bartholomew, now Fitzgerald. Losing a friend in combat is one thing. That's what war's all about. Losing a friend in an accident is something else," I said. "That hurts far more."

"True, and Lieutenant Fitzgerald wasn't the first friend I lost in Korea. Bob Kemmerer, a member of 52-Charlie, lived in the hut next to mine. We ate our meals together; we went to the officers' club together; and we spent hours bullshitting with each other. We were friends.

"One night Kemmerer boarded a C-47 'Gooney Bird' bound for Tokyo being flown by a United Nations pilot from Greece. The tower ordered the Greek to hold clear of the runway so an F-80 loaded with napalm could take off. The Greek pilot misunderstood the tower and pulled on the runway. I watched from a taxi strip as the F-80 sped into the side of the 47. It looked like an atomic bomb went off in front of my eyes. Believe me, the toughest thing about combat isn't flying missions, it isn't even being shot at, it is watching a good friend being killed right in front of you, knowing you are powerless to do anything about it."

"We lost a 29 crew out of Okinawa," I said. " I knew some of their names. I even went to a service for one of them. But I didn't know them well. Maybe God protected me in that way. Maybe, I don't know. What happened after Korea, Warren?"

"I finished my tour and returned to the States, where United Air Lines offered me a job. I had a decision to make: fly the planes I loved for the USAF or fly for United and make a lot more money."

It was an easy decision for Warren Hunt. He stayed in the service, where his career took off with the speed of the planes he flew. The one he loved most was the F-104 Starfighter. It flew at Mach 2.3, more than twice the speed of sound. It had a 54-foot- long fuselage with short seven-foot wings that were so thin you could cut yourself if you rubbed up against them. Hunt was made the command project officer of the 104. He spent most of his career in the air testing planes, hobnobbing with generals, and enjoying himself immensely.

The experiences Warren Hunt had at NASA and Edwards AFB, the stories of the planes he tested and the extraordinary people with whom he worked, would fill the pages of a book twice this size.

Warren Hunt retired a bird colonel with more than 13,000 flying hours—an American hero who made the planes and equipment he tested safer for those who followed, a combat pilot who taught the world how to break an eardrum and fly underwater.

Finally, Bed-Check Charlie Is Laid to Rest

The North Koreans never sent a fighter aircraft below the DMZ. But they did send canvas-and-wood bi-wing planes on nightly missions over our bases in South Korea. The pilots had a few hand grenades and a five-pound lap bomb they would toss over the side. Occasionally they'd hit a plane or a building. They were given the name Bed-Check Charlie and they were more of an irritant than a threat. Nonetheless, many of our pilots tried to shoot them down. But that was almost impossible. A jet could not fly slowly enough to track them and they could turn on a dime while a jet could not.

Warren Hunt told me another tragic story, this one about Bed-Check Charlie.

"My squadron commander, Lieutenant Colonel McHale, and his radar observer, Lieutenant Hostetler, decided one night they were going to bag Bed-Check Charlie. They had to fly very close to Charlie to pick him up because the only part of that old fabric relic that produced a radar blip was the propeller. It had a maximum speed of 80 knots.

"That night McHale in an F-94 cut his speed, got off a burst, and hit Charlie. In his exuberance, he radioed, 'We got him!'

"That was their last transmission. They flew right into the debris field, which knocked them out of the sky. The commies lost one pilot flying a two-bit piece of fabric and we lost an F-94 and two fine officers who between them had ten kids.

"That was the last time anyone tried to get Charlie in a jet. But a Marine Corsair pilot solved the problem. The Corsair had a lower stall speed, was more maneuverable, and could avoid the debris field. The Corsair was the answer to an annoying problem. One Marine pilot shot down five Charlie's and became a Korea ace. From that moment on, Charlie never ventured below the 38th parallel."

Flying Backwards

John Winters on his way to a meeting upstairs.

If Warren Hunt could fly under water, then someone in 52-Charlie had to learn how to fly backwards. That was left to John Winters. Actually, Winters wasn't the first. Pilots learned all about reverse control, a dangerous flight characteristic of the early F-86s. Control reversibility came about when the aircraft approached Mach 1 in a steep dive. At this critical moment, the controls would reverse. Normally if a pilot wanted to dive at a steeper angle, he would push the stick forward, and if he wanted to climb, he would pull back on the stick. But when the F-86A reached Mach .95 the pilot had to pull back on the stick to dive and push the stick forward to climb, which goes against everything you've been taught. The Air Force knew about this flight characteristic, and every F-86A pilot was trained to handle it correctly. "Reverse control" was engineered out of the later models of the 86.

Winters loved the 86 despite its faults. He was assigned to the 51st Fighter Wing at K-13 in Korea, together with several other members of 52-Charlie.

On his seventieth combat mission, while attempting a formation takeoff, Winters' nose-wheel strut collapsed two-thirds of the way down the 8000-foot runway. Winters was forced to abort the takeoff, even though there wasn't enough runway left in which to stop his 86. Fortunately, the field was prepared for this type of an emergency. There was an arresting cable two hundred feet off the end of the runway attached to a heavy anchor chain similar to the ones used on ships. The cable caught Winters' runaway 86 and stopped it. But it also sliced through the exterior fuel tanks, and an immediate flash fire engulfed the plane. Winters sat in the cockpit and watched as the canopy over his head began to melt.

When the fire receded, Winters detonated the ejection seat and was thrown twenty feet sideways. He landed in a large mud puddle and watched as the main fuel tank exploded and his 86 went up in a ball of fire. An ambulance arrived with two medics aboard, who stood staring at the roaring fire. Winters slipped up behind them and heard one of them say to the other, "That guy's a goner!"

Winters tapped him on the shoulder, scaring him half to death, and said, "Are you guys looking for me?"

But that wasn't the most frightening moment of Winters' career in the service. One day while flying a T-33 out of Perrin AFB in Texas, he ran into a violent thunderstorm. St Elmo's fire danced up and down Winters' wings and over his canopy. The altimeter went absolutely crazy—up, then down, then back up as if he were on a high-speed elevator. He bounced all over the sky. Hail hitting his aircraft sounded like a hundred jackhammers. It was black as night inside those clouds and the tops were above 40,000 feet.

The 33 held up and Winters broke out of the clouds, got a fix on the base, and went in for a landing, after which he walked around his plane. It looked as if it had been beaten with a ball-peen hammer; dents covered the entire sheet metal of the fuselage, especially around the engine air intake duct. How the hell he survived that storm he'll never know.

Winters walked away from a fiery 86 with no burns and only a sore back. He learned early in his career how to fly backwards and live, and discovered that a cloud with an anvil on top is not the place to go for a casual day of flying.

Winters and his F-86. A love affair that had an unusual ending.

ASLEEP ON THE JOB

Dick Spaulding prior to one of the most unusual combat missions ever flown.

Dick Spaulding, 52-Charlie, graduated from advanced training at Williams AFB where he got to fly the good stuff, T-33s and F-80s, unlike most other single-engine cadets who completed their training in the T-6. From Williams he was sent to Luke for gunnery instruction and didn't even have to pack his bags, as both bases were in Phoenix.

In August, Dick began his tour of duty in K-2, flying combat with Fuller, McDonnell, and several other members of 52-Charlie. Spaulding kept a diary of each of his first thirty-five missions, and according to him the diary would put an insomniac to sleep.

But oh, the 36th!

Enemy convoys traveled at night with their lights on, and then just before dawn, they'd find a place to hide for the day and turn their lights off. On the night of March 26, 1953, Spaulding and his flight of four 84s were scheduled to make a pre-dawn mission in hopes of catching a convoy running with their lights still on.

The pilots gathered at the flight line. Smith was lead, with Ellis and Dickerson flying two and three. Spaulding flew the slot with the call sign "Red four."

The group had been at altitude for a little more than fifteen minutes when the night turned ugly and death joined Spaulding in the cramped cockpit of his F-84.

Spaulding felt his plane fall off on one wing, and the instrument panel pulsed in and out of focus. He tried to clear his head and regain the altitude he had lost. But just as he did, the plane dove to the right. Something was terribly wrong and Spaulding had no idea what it was. His F-84 had a mind of its own. As quickly as he adjusted to one precipitous move, another occurred. His vision blurred and he found it almost impossible to coordinate his flying. Frustrated and more than a little frightened, he called his leader and explained his problem. Smith ordered Red four back to the base but couldn't accompany him as his group had a mission to fly. They continued on their way to the target.

Spaulding called ground radar for a fix.

Captain Clarence Bell answered Spaulding's call, which might have been the luckiest thing that ever happened to him. Bell had been a pilot in World War II so he not only understand flying but was also one hell of a radar operator.

Spaulding reported that he was confused and needed help.

Bell took over. He informed Spaulding that he was some 90 miles north of the DMZ over enemy territory and asked him to drop his bombs, make a 180-degree turn, and head south. Spaulding failed to respond.

Bell called him again, but there was no answer. Spaulding was in a coma, flying alone over enemy territory without any knowledge of what he was doing.

"Red four, turn your plane 90 degrees to the south. Do you understand?"

There was no answer, but the radar screen showed Red four making a very slow turn in the correct direction.

A moment later, Spaulding blurted something over the command set, which Bell couldn't understand. He sounded drunk and seemed to be in and out of consciousness.

Bell ordered Spaulding to turn south and watched patiently as the plane responded. But then it veered off to the west. He ordered another turn to the south with no response. Spaulding's plane went into a dive and before it recovered, pulled eight g's and popped rivets from the wings and curled the stabilizing fins over the wing tips. His wing tanks were loose and rattling.

Bell was certain something was wrong with Spaulding's oxygen system and that he was dealing with a comatose flyer. He asked Spaulding if he had dumped his bombs as ordered earlier. Spaulding wasn't sure, so Bell ordered him to do so, but then quickly countered that order as Spaulding's F-84 was over Panmunjom where the peace negotiations were taking place. Spaulding would just have to land with those bombs if they were still hanging below the belly of his 84.

Richard Spaulding was unconscious, flying by instinct, reacting to sounds like an automaton. Bell knew he held Spaulding's life in his hands. Somehow he'd have to talk him back to a base in South Korea. That would take the best part of an hour. And when he got him back to that base, he had no idea how he'd get him lined up for a landing.

Bell cajoled and yelled and ordered and screamed at his unconscious charge. It was a rough, a very rough trip. Spaulding's plane bobbed up and down like a cork in the ocean, changing directions every few seconds. Spaulding knew neither where he was nor what he was doing. He was unconscious with his eyes wide open.

Bell realized Spaulding couldn't make it all the way back to K-2, so he decided to vector him to K-13 and pray he had enough instinct to land his plane when he arrived there.

Bell passed Spaulding safely through the mountains surrounding the area. He told Spaulding to add power, take off power, correct right, correct left, lower his rate of descent, increase his rate of descent. Talk! Talk! Talk!

Now came the moment of truth. Bell had done all he could. Spaulding no longer registered on Bell's radar. Spaulding was on his own.

Spaulding grabbed the stick with both hands and forced his eyes open. The tower screamed at him, telling him when to lower his flaps and his gear. He concentrated on one thing only, lining up with that piece of cement in front of him while trying desperately not to pass out again. The tower told him when to level off. Instinctively, he reduced power; the plane touched down on the left wheel first, throwing the plane onto the right wheel. The nose wheel slammed into the cement. Screaming ambulances and fire trucks followed the crippled 84 as it ran off the end of the runway and came to a stop with its nose wheel buried in a bush.

The medics opened the canopy and found that the ejection seat handle had been partially activated. The engine was still idling and Spaulding was hunched over the stick, unconscious. They switched off the engine, pulled Spaulding from the plane, and rushed him to a small medical tent near the flight line.

Somehow, Dick Spaulding had managed to fly a military jet for more than an hour while in a coma. Somehow, he reacted to directions while not having the slightest idea what he was doing. Somehow, he managed to land a plane with his eyes closed, using both hands. Somehow, he managed to kick death out of his cockpit.

Dick Spaulding lived a miracle and Captain Clarence Bell was the man who delivered it to him. To this day, Richard Spaulding doesn't remember hearing a single word Bell spoke. Spaulding's oxygen regulator had failed, which usually means death for a pilot.

The mission he couldn't fly was successful. Smith and his wingmen caught the Korean convoy with their lights on and demolished them.

Spaulding remained on active duty for seven more years. Upon returning to the U.S. he met the Secretary of the Air Force, Eugene Zuckert, and the two became friends. Spaulding was appointed Air Force information officer during the Bay of Pigs and the Cuban missile crisis. He resigned his commission and joined the Air Force reserve where he remained for another 25 years, retiring with the rank of bird colonel.

Today, Dick Spaulding does his sleeping in a bed, but it was not always thus.

Dick Spaulding meets the man who saved his life, Clarence Bell.

One for the Road

This picture of Gil Hasler was actually taken in Korea, not on a back lot in Hollywood.

Gil Hasler had just completed his 100th mission and was biding his time at Squadron OPS when a Mayday call came in. An 86 pilot had just been shot down and the call was for a pickup. The downed pilot, Major Steve Bettinger, a Korean ace with five kills, was a friend of Gil Hasler.

Without a second thought, Hasler asked permission to form a cap. Hasler's tour of duty was over. But like Chuck Levinger and the helicopter pilot who saved Quinn Fuller's life, Hasler did not hesitate to volunteer. That's what the military is all about. If someone is in trouble, you do your damnedest to help even if it means putting your own life at risk.

Permission was given and Hasler contacted three other pilots who without hesitation agreed to fly. The four men boarded their 86s and took off.

In the meantime, the Navy dispatched a Grumman SA 16 Albatross, code-named Dumbo, to affect a water rescue if needed, and the Army sent a helicopter for a ground pickup.

Bettinger had been shot down well north of the 38th parallel so Hasler and his volunteer pilots firewalled their throttles. They had little time to get to their friend.

Bettinger had landed in the sea, and before any of his friends could get to him a North Korean motorboat picked him up. The base called and ordered Hasler to return. All he could do now was pray that Bettinger was alive and would be treated well.

Hasler's 101st combat mission was unsuccessful. But never tell Hasler that or Major Bettinger, who survived his internment and was repatriated after the war.

Most of the missions Hasler flew in Korea were to keep the MiGs from attacking our tactical aircraft: the T-6s, 84s, 51s and 80s. But in doing so, if the opportunity to down a few enemy aircraft availed itself, it was taken.

Each flight of 86s consisted of a flight leader and three wingmen. They would take off, climb to altitude, and fly north. About the time they reached Pyongyang they would drop their wing tanks and prepare for battle. Each mission lasted about an hour-and-a-half, which meant they were on patrol at the Yalu for about forty minutes.

One morning while on patrol at 42,000 feet, Hasler's flight leader,

Major Ayersman, spotted a gaggle of MiGs some three thousand feet above them.

Ayersman wanted a piece of that gaggle. He told his flight to follow and they laddered up the three thousand feet that separated them. In order to keep their speed at an acceptable level, they flew full throttle, then pulled their planes up a thousand feet and flew level until they regained airspeed, then repeated the process.

When they reached 45,000 feet they broke right into the middle of the MiG formation, which appeared to be flying an undisciplined follow-the-leader pattern. Hasler leveled off right next to a MiG. He could have waved to the pilot if he so chose. They flew that way for a few seconds until Ayersman squeezed off a shot at the MiG leader. Parts of that MiG flew off and the mortally wounded plane rolled and began to dive toward the earth.

That was enough for one day. The 86s were outnumbered and flying at an altitude where they were an easy mark for the enemy.

Ayersman called to his flight, "Let's get the hell out of here. Follow me! All four 86s flipped on their backs, dove toward the ground, and headed for home. Ayersman had his first confirmed kill. Gil Hasler had not fired a single shot nor had either of the other two wingmen. Still, they were as responsible for that MiG being shot down as was Major Ayersman and he would be the first to say so.

A short time later Gil Hasler went to war with Major James Jabara, one of the leading aces of all time. Jabara scored kills in both WW II and in Korea. When you're that good, you're paraded around the country selling war bonds and your picture is taken with publicity-seeking congressmen.

Jabara had just returned from a glory trip to the States and was anxious to get back into the fray. Gil Hasler was selected to fly with Jabara and two other 86 pilots. They had just completed their final sweep when Gil spotted four bogeys approaching their flight from 9 o'clock to 6. He alerted Jabara. They turned left, climbed, and pulled in behind two of the MiGs. What Jabara did not realize was that in executing that maneuver, he had placed his flight right in front of the other two MiGs, who were slightly higher and in perfect position to fire on his wingmen.

Jabara fired two bursts and hit the MiG he trailed. The MiG pilot bailed out and the plane nosed downward. But at the same time, Hasler's plane came under heavy fire from both 23 mm and 37 mm cannons. Shells the size of tennis balls and golf balls sailed past his plane, popping like firecrackers as they did so. Under no circumstance should a flight leader endanger his wingmen. Jabara was too fine a pilot to do so. The major simply hadn't seen the other two MiGs. Bad vision is the shortest walk to a mortuary.

When Jabara realized what was happening, he ordered his group to disengage and get the hell out of there. Either those MiG pilots were the worst shots in the world or God was riding co-pilot with Hasler that day. By consensus, Hasler should have been shot down and he knew it.

Jabara scored another victory. Hasler spent the better part of the night in the officers' club under heavy sedation.

The F-86, the preferred plane of Korean ace Jabara and his forgotten wingman, Gil Hasler. The photo is a bit dark; we prefer to think of it as ominous.

Skip Bombing

Peter Orr on his way to create havoc in the north.

I met Peter Orr at a 52-Charlie reunion where he shared some of his combat stories with me, including a unique skip-bombing experience.

Most of the sorties Orr flew were napalm runs or dive-bombing missions. Occasionally, however, OPS would schedule a skip-bombing run. Skip bombing is a little like Bowling for Dollars. The pilot would fly in low and drop a bomb that would skip along the ground before exploding. Skip bombing was used primarily against trains hiding in tunnels.

Peter Orr led a flight of four F-84s on a skip-bombing mission against a tunnel in North Korea. Each aircraft carried two 1000-pound bombs. On their first drop, all four pilots missed the tunnel entirely. On the second pass, Orr flew right up to the mouth of the tunnel before releasing his bomb and then pulled up over the mountain and descended to watch the explosion from the other side.

There was no explosion. Rather Orr's 1000-pound bomb skipped out the other end of the tunnel like a scared jackrabbit, right below his plane.

Orr was about to be blown out of the sky by his own bomb, so he pulled up sharply as his bomb continued into a rice paddy where it blew up, sending rice as far as the eye could see.

Orr told the rest of his flight to save their bombs and look for targets of opportunity. Number three was the first to find a target: an ammo truck wandering aimlessly along a mountain road. He strafed the truck, which disappeared in a ball of fire and smoke.

Number four found a bridge spanning two mountains, which was used by the enemy as a supply route. He dropped his second bomb on the bridge, but it fell well short and hit the mountain. Suddenly there was a cataclysmic eruption as the whole side of the mountain disappeared. He'd hit an ammo dump and a fuel area. Sometimes it's better to be lucky than good.

On another day, Peter Orr was on a dive-bombing mission well north of the Yalu River. On such a mission, the pilot begins his attack at altitude by diving towards the target. When he pulls out of his dive at about two-to-three-thousand feet, he raises the nose of his aircraft and it creates a negative G, which automatically releases his bomb. Well, on this particular mission it did not automatically release and because of the weight of the bombs the plane did not pull out of the dive as it was supposed to. By the time Orr could manually release his bombs he was at treetop level. A second later he would have been in the ground. He remembers vividly seeing a North Korean man running along the ground in front of his aircraft. That's too damn low.

"I learned something that day," Peter told me. "I learned that on any future mission I would manually release my bombs. That may not have been SOP (standard operating procedure) with the Air Force, but it was SOP with me."

Peter Orr returned to Luke AFB as an instructor following his combat tour. They were training foreign pilots at Luke. On three different occasions, one of these students damn near rammed Orr in the air. That's when he decided he had another calling.

Peter Orr retired from the Air Force and went through dental school. After forty yeas as a dentist Dr. Orr has finally put aside his drills and today breeds cattle on his ranch in Missouri.

Special delivery with Dr. Peter Orr's fondest wishes. You can be sure this bomb was manually released.

The Shack by the Track

Lt Col. Bill Pearce retired with a Silver Star, 4 DFCs, 19 air medals, and the eternal thanks of a young lady and young man in North Korea.

Peter Orr wasn't the only member of 52-Charlie flying tunnel missions. Bill Pearce often tried his hand at skip bombing with about the same success. On an early mission, he led a flight of four F-84s, armed with two 1000-pound bombs each. Their target: a train tunnel. All eight bombs were dropped and all eight bombs missed the target.

Pearce decided to fly to the other side of the mountain in the hope that a train might exit the tunnel. But there was no train, only a small shack beside the track. Pearce decided to blow the hell out of that shack. He began a strafing run, his finger on the trigger. Just as he was about to shoot, a young girl dashed out of the shack, her skirt and blouse askew, followed by a young man trying desperately to button his pants as he ran for his life.

"I couldn't shoot them," he told me during an evening we spent at a bar. "All I could do was laugh and wonder if their spouses knew about the small shack on the other side of the mountain."

Pearce flew 107 combat missions in the F-84 and all of them during the day. That changed, however, when his commander, Colonel Ellis, assembled a night-flight team, which included Larry Gardner, Chappy McDonnell, and Bill Pearce.

"We would fly at night when the moon was up, Ted. If it was bright enough we could spot enemy trucks running without their lights, and they were easy targets. These were fun missions, until one night the fun disappeared."

"This sounds interesting," I said.

"Interesting isn't the right word. This particular night the moon wasn't up. I wasn't watching my altimeter but I remember seeing a low deck of clouds and decided that I'd drop through those clouds to see if I could pick up a truck or two. But something held me back. Thank God for that something. That was not a bank of clouds it was ground fog. If I had flown through that it would have been all over in an instant."

"It pays to check the altimeter from time to time. Did you ever run into a MiG, Bill?"

"Yeah, one. I was flying near the Yalu at twenty angels or so (20,000 feet) when I spotted a MiG on his way back to Antung. He didn't see me. The 84 could never catch a MiG, they were much faster, but I could dive down on him and certainly get some shots away. This was going to be my claim to fame. What I didn't see were two F-86s trailing the MiG. One went by me in a whoosh and shot the poor bastard down. I was pissed. My moment to shine and that asshole in the 86 stole it from me. Afterwards, the pilot pulled up to my 84 and I gave him the finger and returned to base. That's as close as I ever came to hero status.

"You want to know what my most frightening missions were?"

"Absolutely!"

"They were five missions I flew in Germany as a bombardier in WW II. The target of those missions was Berlin. The Germans had pulled virtually all the guns back to protect the city. And when we flew over, the flak was so thick you could walk on it. Those were the most frightening moments of my life."

"That's understandable. Did you ever get hit in Korea, Bill?"

"A few times. Lots of flak scars but nothing serious until my final mission. Colonel Ellis asked me to join him and two others in attacking a bridge in Pyongyang. Up to this point, Pyongyang was an open city, off-limits to UN bombing. The suburbs were fair game, but the city itself was not. The enemy knew it and made no attempt to shoot at Ellis. But after Ellis and his two wingmen had released their bombs, the defenders got busy on the remaining plane in the formation. Me. They threw everything at me except the deed to the city. I was hit, but I could still control my plane. I dropped my bombs and returned to base."

"How'd you guys do?"

"Sorry you asked. Not a single bomb hit the target, but I did have the distinction of dropping the very last bomb of the war on the capital of North Korea."

In summary: Peter Orr and Bill Pearce claimed for their flights a rice paddy, an ammo truck, the side of a mountain, the interruption of a lovers' tryst, various patches of ground leading up to a bridge in an open city, a complete miss of a target in Pyongyang, and an almost MiG.

Before Pearce finished his Korean tour, he met one of his lifelong idols and helped save his life. Pearce was flying near the Yalu River when he received word that a Marine pilot needed help. He ordered his wingmen to return to the base, as they were running low on fuel, and told them he'd hang around for a few minutes to see if he could find the troubled plane.

It didn't take long. It was a Navy F-9-F Panther jet trailing smoke. Only skilled flying and a bit of luck would get that plane back to our side of the line. Pearce tried to contact the Marine pilot but failed. He flew alongside the stricken aircraft and with hand signals instructed the pilot to follow him.

It'd take twenty minutes to get to a friendly field and Pearce wasn't sure the Panther jet could last that long. It was smoking and losing altitude. Pearce tucked his wing under that of the wounded bird and did his best through hand signals to assure the pilot they were going to make it. When they were in sight of the field, Pearce pointed it out and waved goodbye. He took off for K-2 dangerously low on fuel.

The Marine pilot flew a straight-in pattern.

Paul Savage, also a member of 52-Charlie, was returning from a mission. He'd just entered the downwind leg of the traffic pattern when he saw the F-9-F preparing to land. It was a ball of flame from the cockpit aft. If the Panther jet didn't clear the runway on landing, the tower would have to close the runway.

Savage knew his flight didn't have the fuel to make a go-around. They had to land. They had no other option. Land or crash and face the consequences.

John Winters had touched down just before the Marine entered the pattern and was taxiing to his hard stand. To get there he had to cross the active runway. The tower told him to hold until the F-9-F passed him. The Panther jet crashed with its wheels up, throwing sparks and flames into the air. As it skidded towards Winters' plane, it began spraying bullets. The pilot had forgotten to switch off his guns when he left the combat zone. Bullets were flying everywhere and Winters was powerless to do a thing. He could not move his aircraft. He called on his guardian angel and prayed that the bullets would miss his 86.

The plane slid past Winters and came to a stop just far enough off the edge of the runway for the fuel-starved F-80s to land. The pilot turned off the guns, exited the aircraft, and ran away from the burning ship.

Meanwhile Savage had turned onto final. Paul had seen more than his share of ground fire and tracers and crashing planes. But at that moment he was more concerned about the runway than about what was happening on it. He had to use that valuable piece of property and he had to use it right now.

Warren Hunt was on mobile control that day and cleared the F-9-F to land. He had advised the pilot to bail out, but the Marine's radio was out and he never got the message.

The tower never closed the runway. All of the F-80s made it down safely. But a few inches here or there and a lot of pilots may have lost their lives that day.

And who was the pilot on the doomed F-9-F?

The Splendid Splinter, the pride of the Boston Red Sox. None other than Ted Williams.

Ted Williams landed a fatally wounded plane and only an extraordinary pilot could have put that craft down and walked away. Williams was as good in the air as he was on a playing field. Everyone who witnessed that incident said that Williams should have bailed out. What he did was irresponsible. But the Panther jet has a confined cockpit and those who flew it knew that if they had to bail out they had more than an even chance of having their kneecaps damaged beyond repair. Williams never discussed why he made the decision he did. It can only be assumed he wasn't going to impair his chances of returning someday to the green monster in Fenway Park.

The Boston fans owe a great debt of thanks to four members of 52-Charlie, without whom Ted Williams may never have returned to Boston. Paul Savage, Bill Pearce, Warren Hunt, and John Winters.

Savage and Hunt met with Williams in the officers' club shortly thereafter and a good deal of Scotland's finest was consumed.

The next day Ted Williams called Pearce to thank him. In the fifty-plus years since the Korean War, we have had many class reunions. The day that Ted Williams crashed at K-13 may well have been the first.

The F-9-F—Ted Williams crashed one in Korea.

Snafu—It's a Military Thing

Paul Savage on his way to meet another celebrity. That may account for the crooked smile on his face.

Paul Savage enjoyed his drink with Ted Williams, but he was about to meet a celebrity with whom he would not enjoy drinking. Savage had just returned from a mission when General Glenn Barcus's adjutant met him at the flight line. Barcus was in charge of everything that had wings in Korea, and, according to his adjutant, was investigating the mission Paul Savage had just completed.

A few United Nations troops had been wounded by American ordnance which had fallen short of its target in an area where Paul Savage dropped his bombs. Mistakes happen in every war; men are wounded, sometimes killed, by their own troops; a bomb mistakenly falls on a civilian site. A one-second delay in releasing a bomb can be devastating, but men and machines are fallible and those fallibilities can lead to death.

Still, when a bomb falls where it shouldn't, there's hell to pay. It's the kind of story a congressman might latch on to.

Savage, his wing commander, his group commander, his squadron commander and his Mosquito spotter were flown to Barcus's headquarters in Seoul for a "discovery" session. Translation: determine whose ass was going to be hung out to dry.

The general was pleasant but firm. Savage and his Mosquito pilot assured the general they'd hit their target, but it was difficult to prove. Paul Savage's career was on hold. Meanwhile the Army initiated its own investigation and determined that an errant artillery shell caused the accident. In the military you are guilty until proven innocent. Some call that SNAFU, or Situation Normal, All Fucked Up.

Savage and his entourage were absolved and returned to duty. He had an excellent combat record so he was offered a perk, the option to fly a few solo night missions. He thought it could be fun, so he accepted, not realizing how dangerous a night mission can be when you are flying below mountain peaks.

The North Koreans moved equipment at night, often with their lights on. If they heard a plane's engine, all lights were turned off.

The pilot flying the dive-bombing run had a preset target in his mind and would dive to 3000 feet before releasing his ordnance. This was a bit tricky as there were unseen mountains higher than 3000 feet in the area. The Koreans often turned on searchlights to further confuse the pilot. And if the pilot was not mindful of the situation, he could dive into a mountain or the ground. It was not the best of all worlds.

Flying at night was supposed to be a perk for having successfully completed fifty missions. Reward hell, it was an invitation to an early eulogy. After seven night flights Savage wisely decided he was no more interested in going out on the town at night than he was in meeting celebrities.

Baby, It's Cold Outside

Don Monchil and the plane he hated, the F-51. That's understandable, as it tried to kill him twice.

Don Monchil graduated in the class of 52-Charlie. Following cadets, Monchil was checked out in the F-51 Mustang, a plane he absolutely hated. He was convinced that the 51 was put on this earth to kill him, if not in training certainly in combat. And it did everything in its power to do so.

Monchil went to gunnery school at Luke, where pilots were being killed by the numbers. On one day, an F-84 had a midair collision with a B-26 that was towing the gunnery target. All were killed. Luke lost at least eight pilots within a week.

From Luke, Monchil was posted to Johnson AFB near Tokyo. His assignment: fly F-51s with Republic of Korea markings to Korea and turn them over to poorly trained ROK pilots, who according to Monchil immediately went out and killed themselves.

On one such mission, Monchil was over the ocean when his coolant line burst, spraying coolant all over the canopy and making it almost impossible to see. Without coolant, the engine would seize and the plane would augur in.

Monchil managed to get rid of the canopy and actually started to climb out on the wing in order to bail out. He had one leg in the cockpit and one foot on his wing when he saw whitecaps far below and no vessels within sight. It was January and Monchil wanted no part of that ocean. He climbed back into his 51, despite being buffeted by the three-hundred-mile-per-hour slipstream. He pulled off power, enriched the mixture to lower the cylinder-head temperatures, and increased the pitch of the prop. That put as little strain on the engine as possible. Now the question was, could he nurse that wounded bird back to land?

There was an old Japanese airfield adjacent to a beach. It hadn't been used since the war ended. Bomb craters still dotted the field. But Monchil knew it was his only hope. The field had grass runways. This must have been his finest hour. He made the field and successfully put his plane down, running in and out of craters that had been there for seven years. He never saw that 51 again.

But he was given a replacement, much to his chagrin. One morning he lined up for takeoff carrying a live 500-pound bomb and racks of rockets below his wings. His wing tanks were topped off. He was just below red-line weight. The tower cleared him and he shoved his throttle forward. Just as he broke ground, at the most critical time of flight, his engine quit. He had used up the entire runway. There was virtually no runoff at Johnson AFB. Instead he stared at a rock river that meant instant death.

Suddenly the engine caught and he nursed the plane up a few feet. Once again it quit, than caught again. This pattern continued. Just when Monchil was convinced he was going to die the engine started once more.

He reached a thousand feet and now it was time to land without power before his engine quit for good. At Johnson AFB, pilots were required to make a right turn out of traffic and re-enter the pattern on the downwind leg. At that moment, Monchil was thinking only about getting his plane back on the ground and the shortest way to do that was by turning left and flying directly over the field.

The gods were with him that day, or at least until he landed, when all hell broke loose. His commanding officer roared down the runway in a jeep and met Monchil, screaming at the top of his lungs.

Monchil had turned over the base with a sick airplane and enough ordnance to blow that base and all who were on it to kingdom come. He remembered seeing people on the ground pointing at his aircraft while running as fast as they could to a bunker.

He saved a plane. He saved his life. But he endured the invective of an officer who really knew how to use invective.

Monchil is one of the few pilots from WW II and Korea who absolutely hated the Mustang. And he hasn't changed his mind in the past fifty years. A good friend of his and member of 52-Charlie, John Cottingham, on the other hand says the 51 was the best plane he ever flew and he remained in the service for thirty-six years, retiring as a bird colonel.

Here's Monchil flying pretty good formation in the plane he hated.

Cottingham wasn't lucky enough to fly combat, but he was posted to the Pentagon for a number of years carrying books for generals. That's enough combat for anyone. Cottingham told me he was an "almost ace," having bailed out twice from crippled aircraft. To become an ace you must destroy three enemy aircraft. Cottingham destroyed only two and they were ours. Cottingham was trained in F-80s and flew many other jets. But even today, his favorite plane is still the old F-51 Mustang.

Watch Out, Chester Is in the Neighborhood

Charles Chester made flying an adventure wherever he was. Most others, though, didn't want to be part of that adventure.

After graduating from cadets, Charles Chester went through gunnery school, checked out in the F-86, and was sent to Kimpo in South Korea. There he spent much of his time courting disaster along with many of the other pilots in his group.

On one such mission, Chester and his flight of four aircraft were returning from the Yalu. All were desperately short of fuel. Chester had landed and the other four 86s had just entered the pattern when a fifth 86 called in a Mayday.

Bruno Giordano, a West Point graduate and a close friend of Chester's, had stayed over the target far too long. His engine had flamed out from fuel starvation while still over enemy territory. Bruno called mobile control and said he could make the field but he would have to land downwind. He didn't have enough altitude to glide to the other end of the runway.

Mobile ordered the other four jets on final to go around so that Bruno could land.

"Negative. We haven't enough fuel to go around. Tell the other guy to bail out."

Bruno didn't want to test his silk that day so he asked the 86 pilots if they would land on the right side of the runway and he would land on the left. They agreed. What happened next is something that even the famous Air Force Thunderbird team wouldn't try. The flight of four, flying into the wind, touched down at one end of the runway while Bruno touched down at the other end going in the opposite direction.

Bruno passed the other four aircraft about the center of the runway with a closure rate of more than three hundred knots. Chester said it was the damnedest sight he had ever seen as the five jets passed each other head-on.

Charles Chester flew 70 combat missions, most of which were near the Yalu River. He often mixed it up with MiGs. Once while flying with his wingman, Jimmy Pearce, he was jumped by two MiGs. Chester broke right and got on the tail of one of the MiGs. He fired his guns and got hits on the enemy's fuselage, wings, and tail surfaces. He'd emptied his guns and had to return.

After he broke off, Pearce reported that the MiG was trailing smoke and was losing altitude. Chester was given a probable.

He always seemed to be around when the unusual took place. On another mission Chester was flying at 35,000 feet when he noticed his tachometer was reading zero. That's not a happy sign. He assumed the gauge was broken. A few minutes later his oil pressure indicator read zero. Now he knew he was in trouble. The engine started to grind and shake. The only way to keep the engine from seizing was to run at one hundred percent power. He made it to Kimpo at 25,000 feet, but he had to retard his airspeed to land. He stop-cocked the throttle and set up a flameout pattern, and the engine seized as expected.

Chester said that he was Mr. Cool coming in for the landing, or at least he pretended to be. K-14 had a drag restraint at the end of the runway to catch runaway planes. On base leg he asked mobile to activate it and told them he would land down the runway a bit to be sure he hit cement, not dirt. He brought his dead aircraft to a stop with a third of the runway left.

"No sweat," Chester said to his friend, Jimmy Pearce. "It was a walk in the park."

"Walk in the park, huh?" Jimmy said. "Why then, Charlie, were you transmitting all the way down final? Was your thumb frozen on the mike button, Mr. Cool? You know, you sounded like a dog in heat. I have never heard anyone breathing that hard. But as you said, 'No Sweat!'"

Charles got out of the service in 1957 and went to law school. But he loved to fly so he joined the Air National Guard, where more excitement awaited him. He was on a training flight in a KC-97 tanker with three other pilots. It was a very cold night and he and a friend were sitting on gasoline heaters in the back of the aircraft, waiting their time to fly the last half of the mission. Chester was not wearing his seatbelt. The pilots were shooting touch-and-gos at Amon Carter field in Texas.

Chester remembers that on the third touch-and-go the engine sounded strange and he had a sense that their airspeed was too low. Something was the matter.

Just before the runway was a thirty-foot drop-off, and as the KC-97 approached, it hit the hill before the runway. The fuselage broke in two and immediately caught fire. The heaters that Charles was sitting over exploded and the entire rear fuselage was burning. There were two emergency exits in the rear, one on the right, one on the left. The right exit was billowing fire. Charles and his friend managed to jump out of the left exit before the whole plane was engulfed in flame.

Chester's hands were badly burned and required grafting. He spent eight weeks in a burn center.

Charles Chester retired from the Air National Guard after 26 years of service with the rank of Lieutenant Colonel. He is one fine lawyer and when he decides to retire from the law, with the experiences he had in the air he could become a ride at Disneyland

Out of This World

Jim McDivitt, combat pilot, test pilot, aeronautical engineer, astronaut, CEO, and board member.

Most of us are content to enjoy the boundaries of our planet, to live our lives within the confines of that which we know. There are of course a small number of men and women whose curiosity is never satisfied, whose every day is tomorrow and whose tomorrows are every day. They are men like Columbus, Magellan, and Vespucci. Men with the restless minds of an Edison and an Einstein. They are dreamers like Madame Curie and Galileo. They are unfettered pilots like General James McDivitt.

McDivitt began his flight training at Moultrie, Georgia, where he slipped on a T-6 and took possession of the sky. That was the day McDivitt began to move along an unbroken path, where every adventure was uncharted, every experience untested. From the moment he soloed, his heart and his soul would forever be ten thousand feet above the ground.

McDivitt completed his pilot training at Williams AFB in Arizona and got a free taxi ride across Phoenix to Luke where he transitioned into F-80s. He loved the 80 and was looking forward to being checked out in the 86. But the Air Force had other plans for him. They needed F-84 pilots in Korea. So McDivitt was given the mandatory ten hours of flight instruction in the 84 and declared proficient. While he waited for orders to send him to Korea he and a couple of other pilots expressed their frustration at having to fly the 84, a plane they disliked.

One of those officers said he had a cousin who was a private in the processing line and perhaps he could get their orders changed. It turned out he could.

Jim got the orders he sought and was sent to K-13 in Korea to fly combat in F-80s and later F-86s, planes he loved. The normal tour of duty in Korea for a fighter pilot was 100 missions. That was the day every combat pilot looked forward to. Almost every pilot. Not Jim McDivitt. As he neared the end of his tour, McDivitt re-upped. He put in for an additional 25 and following that another 25. And by the time the war ended, McDivitt had flown 145 combat missions. All of those were ground-support missions. In his 145 combat sorties, he never engaged a MiG, never fired at an enemy aircraft. But he saw plenty of ground fire.

The F-80—Jim McDivitt's first love in Korea.

On one flight over Pyongyang, McDivitt was hit by flak and his elevator and horizontal stabilizer were badly damaged. The elevator controls the altitude of the aircraft. The horizontal stabilizer controls yaw. Most pilots would have headed for home or bailed out. Not McDivitt. He had his plane trimmed perfectly so that he could adjust altitude by adding or taking off power. So the first thing McDivitt did was to find a target for his bombs, lower his craft to a better bombing altitude, and drop his bombs. Then and only then he headed for home.

Flying a plane without an elevator and with a badly disfigured horizontal stabilizer is difficult enough, but landing it is next to impossible. Jim McDivitt never gave it a thought. He was sure he had the skills to guide his F-86 to a safe landing. And he was right. Jim landed his plane using his speed brakes, his gear, and his power to adjust his altitude.

Jim was happiest when he was in the air—a natural-born pilot. When the squadron needed a flight leader, it came as no surprise that McDivitt was the choice. Unfortunately McDivitt's rank was not up to his talent, and that caused the occasional problem. One afternoon, two squadrons from his base were scheduled to fly a mission together, eight planes. Major John Bell and Lieutenant Jim McDivitt were the

Jim McDivitt and what remained of the elevator on his F-86. Landing this plane would test the skill of the very best.

leaders of the two squadrons. At the appointed time, McDivitt had his flight start their engines and wait for the major to taxi to the runway. He waited and waited, and finally he had his flight shut their engines down to conserve fuel. He was about to order his planes refueled when he spotted the major walking slowing to his aircraft.

McDivitt now had a decision to make, refuel or pray they had enough fuel to get back safely. His decision was made for him. Bell's flight took the runway and McDivitt's flight was forced to follow. He did not have time to refuel.

They completed the mission successfully, but the four planes in McDivitt's flight landed on fumes. Luckily a disaster was averted.

He was pissed. He jumped out of his aircraft and ran to Major Bell's plane and told him exactly what he thought. It is not a good idea to chew out someone two grades above you in rank. But if that scared you, you'd never get off the space pad.

In June of 1953, Jim McDivitt ran out of war and it was time to return to the States. He was posted to Bangor, Maine, and spent thirteen months in God's icebox. Thirteen months shoveling walks and deicing wings.

In 1957 McDivitt attended the aeronautical engineering school at the University of Michigan under the auspices of the USAF. He graduated number one in his class.

He was now a much-sought-after pilot with an excellent combat record and a unique education.

If you have those skills, you may just end up at Edwards AFB as a test pilot in one of the most dangerous jobs in the military. Jim McDivitt was qualified in every respect and he wanted to fly the planes that were still on the drawing board.

McDivitt tested the new T-38, the F-100, and the F-104. His favorite was the 104. "It was a bit skittish and you had to keep one step ahead of the airplane, but it was wonderful to fly."

A bit skittish indeed! McDivitt told me the story of how he crashed a 104 and walked away from it.

Jim McDivitt crash-landed a 104 at Edwards and the base threw a party for him that night.

"My 104 had just completed a maintenance check and I was required to test fly it before it could be put back on flying status. I took off with a full load of fuel. The plane handled beautifully. It was a great day for flying and my fuel tanks were full, so I decided to fly to the supersonic corridor and take the 104 to Mach 2.

"At Mach 1.5 all hell broke loose. I could no longer control the stick, which pulsed from left to right then back again. The plane was all over the sky. I pulled off the power and as the plane slowed the rolling stopped. Now I had a decision to make: bail out or try to land the crippled aircraft."

"I'd bet my bottom dollar that you chose to stay with the plane," I said.

"You're right. I was sure I could handle the situation so I decided to land the thing. The runway at Edwards was 15,000 feet long and it had an overrun. That's enough runway to land any plane there is. I knew I would have to bring it in at 200-plus knots due to the fuel load. But I had done that before. I entered the pattern and completed my landing check. But…! And this was a big but."

"But what?"

"But as I applied power to reach landing speed, the vibrations began anew. I could not control the stick. It flew from one side to the other. Personally I don't think there's a man strong enough to have held that stick in one position. I was in trouble and I knew it. The plane was out of control and I was too damn low to bail out, but still I was not overly concerned."

"Why am I not surprised?"

"I figured I had a chance, and a good one. I flew the 104 into the runway and as I hit the ground, one wheel collapsed and tucked under my wing. The plane was still rolling from left to right and the rolling became so severe that first one wing tip hit the runway, then the other, and so on. I pulled off the power and the rolling stopped but I couldn't control the direction of the 104. It slid off the runway into the desert and hit a sand dune and then a second dune. Finally it skidded to a stop. I got out of that plane as fast as I could. The tanks were bulging with fuel. All it would take to blow it up was a spark. Fortunately there was no spark, so after a couple of minutes I got back in and reinserted the pins in the ejection seat so no one would get hurt."

"You got back in a plane that had just crashed and had full fuel tanks? Was that absolutely necessary?"

"No, but someone would have to do it eventually. Why not me?"

Why not McDivitt indeed? The 104 was repaired and used as a non-flying rocket-powered aircraft in the test pilot school.

There is a tradition at Edwards that if a pilot crashes a plane and lives, they have a party. McDivitt had one hell of a party that night and was flying again in the morning.

McDivitt's career now began in earnest. He spent six weeks preparing to fly the X-15 rocket ship and at about the same time applied for the space program at NASA. Just as he was about to fly the X-15 the NASA assignment came through. In September of 1962 McDivitt reported to Houston with eight other future astronauts. The Mercury program was in its final phase and the Gemini program was about to begin. After two years of training, Jim McDivitt and Ed White flew into space together in a Gemini capsule. During that mission White would become the first astronaut to walk in space. The two astronauts orbited the earth sixty-six times.

This EVA (extra-vehicular activity) was not without incident. When White returned to the capsule the hatch wouldn't close. That was a concern. McDivitt wrestled with it for what seemed to be an eternity before he finally managed to get it locked.

On January 26, 1967, Jim McDivitt lost his best friend, Ed White. Astronauts White, Grissom, and Chaffee were doing a countdown demonstration test in the Apollo 1 craft when a flash fire consumed the capsule and killed the three astronauts.

McDivitt was in California when he heard the news of Ed's death. He had flown his own plane to the coast, but he was so distraught that he left his plane there and returned to Houston on a commercial flight. He was named summary courts officer for Ed White. It became his responsibility to make all the arrangements and to comfort the family. It was the toughest job McDivitt had in his entire military career.

On March 3, 1969, Jim McDivitt, David Scott, and Russell Schweickart were shot into space aboard Apollo 9 for a ten-day orbital flight. During this flight the lunar module would be tested in space for the first time.

McDivitt and Schweickart crawled into the module, undocked, and drifted some 200 miles from the Apollo 9. The LM did not have a heat shield so it was imperative that they re-dock. Once the tests were completed, McDivitt and Schweickart guided the LM back to the spacecraft and became the first astronauts to successfully re-dock in space.

McDivitt was next appointed manager of the Apollo space program. He served as the Apollo manager for flights 12,13,14,15, and 16. He was the man in charge when they brought Apollo 13 back from space against odds.

Jim McDivitt, an American icon: a test pilot, a combat pilot, and an astronaut who served his country in and out of this world. After twenty extraordinary years in the Air Force and NASA, Jim retired to civilian life where he became executive vice president of Consumers Power in Michigan, president of Pullman Standard division, and a senior vice president of Rockwell International. Today he serves on several boards, is an advisor to the University of Michigan, and is involved in charitable affairs.

Letters Home

Larry Gardner (third from the right) with his flight group including Quinn Fuller (far left). Larry did everything in the air a pilot could possibly do except fly into space and had he been two inches shorter he'd have done that.

Larry Gardner began his flying career in 1943 when he enlisted in the Army Air Force at the age of seventeen. Howie Pierson, Warren Henderson, Max Hanson, Bill Vogel, Harold Cobb, Ralph Mackey,

Bill Pearce, and Larry Gardner had two things in common: They were members of 52-Charlie and they all served in WW II.

Gardner's first combat mission in WW II was as a gunner on a B-24. Their target: the oil refinery plants at Ploesti, considered the most dangerous mission of the war. One-third of the crews who flew this mission were lost.

During his tour of duty in Europe Gardner had a finger shot off when an enemy shell ripped through his turret. He was also shot down behind enemy lines. There he hid in a hollowed-out log infested with spiders, which Gardner hated before he was discovered by Italian partisans who returned him to the Allies.

In 1951 Larry Gardner applied for aviation cadets and was assigned to 52-Charlie as a student officer. He became one of its most distinguished pilots. He went to primary at Columbus, advanced at Williams, and jet gunnery training at Luke. Then he was posted to the 8th Fighter/Bomber squadron at K-2 in Taegu, where he would fly one hundred combat missions. Gardner was married shortly before he was sent to Korea and he documented each combat mission he flew with a letter to Clare, his bride. Clare kindly sent me copies of Larry's letters. I have selected for inclusion in this book those that I believe best describe the perils of combat and the drama of life and death in the air war over Korea.

December 6, 1952 6th Mission

I thought this was going to be my last mission. We hit troop concentrations west of Wonsan. Everything was fine until I started to come off my bomb run and found that my stick would only go back about two inches. I had a 3000-foot mountain right in front of me. I threw in full back trim and it helped but I still wasn't going to make it over that mountain. I was about to eject when I saw a crevice in the mountain and I turned into it. Right then I didn't think I'd make it so I dropped my dive doors and it flipped my nose up and I mushed through the tops of the trees. I climbed and when I released the backpressure it was fine so I came home with only a few scratches from the trees on the bottom of the fuselage and wings.

January 21, 1953 20th Mission

My plane Tippy II didn't last too long. One of the pilots on a night mission was flying my plane when an oxygen regulator failed and he got hypoxia. He lost control of the plane but bailed out. Tippy II was spread out over two square miles on a mountain next to the base. The pilot was not hurt and is scheduled to resume combat in a week's time. I have some bad news, honey. One of my classmates in 52-Charlie, Lindsay Bartholomew, was killed when his plane crashed on the 7th of January. Lindsay and I were good friends. I will miss him.

March 23, 1953 55th Mission.

Last night I led the mission. Our objective: targets of opportunity. We got two trucks right off. It looked like it was going to be a great night until we reached Yangdoh, that's where John Corbett (52-Charlie) got it and where I was hit earlier. In their marshalling yard I saw five passenger train cars and about twenty-five boxcars. But it looked like a flak trap so I told the flight to climb and look it over. As we flew over, they opened up with everything they had. For the next half hour, we really caught hell. We were continuously in and out of heavy flak.

Quinn Fuller got boxed in a flak trap and couldn't get out. I gave Quinn directions but he was having one hell of a time. Finally he did get out with minor damage to his wing. When we got back we were wet with perspiration and had a slight case of the clanks. It was the worst mission I ever had.

March 28, 1953 61st Mission

Yesterday our Deputy Wing Commander, Colonel Evans, was shot down at "Old Baldy"—he bailed out and they saw him taken prisoner.

I also had a five-minute rat race with a bandit. I chased him all over but I lost him in between some hill about three hundred feet off the deck. I was low on fuel so I broke it off. But going home I had my closest call. I was climbing and leveled off at 33,000 feet. I was in the soup, on instruments, when suddenly the canopy blew open and broken glass flooded the cockpit. It [the wind stream] caught me by the shoulder and wedged me between the seat and the canopy. I was doing 450 knots and the temperature was fifty degrees below zero. The wind stream tore my oxygen mask from my face and my eyes watered from the cold. When the canopy blew I must have pulled back on the stick, the plane stalled and went into a spin. All the instruments were spinning and I was pinned in. I tried to get the canopy closed but I couldn't reach the switch and the ejection seat won't work with the canopy opened. I screamed toward earth. I cut the throttle and dropped the dive brakes to lower my rate of descent. I even undid my seat belt and tried to jump out but the "G" force held me in plus I couldn't get my arm loose. Then a miracle. The instruments all became clear. I brought it out of the spin on instruments. I had lost 12,000 feet in less than a minute. But it seemed like a year. I put my oxygen mask back on and worked my arm loose. I finally got the canopy closed. I had to fly another forty-five minutes on instruments back to the base. I was never so glad to get on the ground. It took ten minutes to get out of the cockpit. My left sleeve of my flight suit and survival suit had ripped off.

April 9, 1953 68th Mission

I led an early light reccy and we did as much damage with four planes as a twelve-ship group could do. On one of my strafing passes I got a 37 mm shell right in the dive door section. I was in a vertical bank about 500 feet off the deck when Wham-O my hydraulic system shot right out of the plane and with it my aileron boost. With both arms and legs I got it straightened out and headed for Wonsan harbor in case I had any other trouble. My emergency gear extension system worked so I had no trouble landing. I was lucky… my high-pressure filter was pushed in but didn't leak. If it had leaked, it would have started a fire and probably an explosion. I have the shell fragment. Keeping it as a good luck piece.

Then came the afternoon mission near the Yalu. I was chasing a Jeep down the road and I dropped a 1000 pound combination bomb and I blew three holes in my rear end. One piece cut two holes in my engine shrouding and two combustion chambers. This was strictly my own fault. I got the Jeep but I would sure have felt silly having dinner on the Yalu as a result of my own bomb blast. Some sad news. Billy Graham, 52-Charlie, bought the farm. As far as I know he was hit and went for one of our friendly islands. In an effort to save the plane, he tried to land on the beach. He just blew up or burned, either way he didn't get out.

Following his tour of duty in Korea, Larry Gardner served with the CIA in Bangkok, where he was a fighter pilot advisor to the Royal Thailand Air Force and flew many covert operations throughout Asia. He became a test pilot at Edwards Air Force base and then flew another one hundred combat missions in Vietnam, earning the Silver Star, our nation's third highest honor.

Altogether, Larry Gardner flew more than three hundred combat missions in three major wars before he was forty years old. He was shot. He was shot down. He was shot up and he lived through the most frightening moments a pilot could imagine.

The only thing Gardner didn't accomplish in the air was to fly into space. Upon his return from Vietnam, he was slated for the Apollo program, but unfortunately, he was too tall and therefore disqualified.

Larry Gardner was an American hero. He died on July 8, 1999, and was buried in Arlington National Cemetery with full military honors.

The Dark Side of Friendship

Jackie Stewart, the famous Formula One race driver, was a sensitive young man who admitted he had few friends on the circuit. There was a reason for that—early in his driving career he lost a close friend in a Formula One race. He could not stand the pain that caused and made a conscious decision not to get too close to any other driver.

As a combat pilot, you cannot avoid others in your flight. You bunk with them, you eat with them, you drink with them, you play with them, and the thing that gets you through the hell of war is friendship. But there is a dark side.

Grady Hinson, 52-Charlie, bunked with Peter Orr. They were close friends. When Peter returned from his skip-bombing mission, he learned that he had been posted to fly the next day, which pleased him. But his friend Grady Hinson wanted to add to his mission number so he could rotate home and asked Peter to swap assignments. Grady was scheduled to fly to Tokyo to pick up a new plane and remain overnight while there, and Grady had a compelling offer:

"I'll fly your combat mission, Peter, you go to Tokyo and have a night on the town."

Now that sounded pretty good to Peter. So they went to Colonel Jones to see if they could exchange orders. The colonel wouldn't go for it. The orders were already cut and Grady was to go to Japan.

Grady turned to Peter and said, "Grady, have a good trip."

Peter responded, "Peter, have a good mission."

Colonel Jones turned to the two men and said, "You wouldn't do that, would you?"

"What will you do, send us home?"

The colonel smiled and agreed to have the first sergeant change the orders.

The next day Peter took off for Japan. He had just registered at the Nitkatsu Hotel when he received a phone call from OPS in Kusan. Grady had been killed on the mission.

Hinson was a rock-solid fighter pilot He had been leading a strike with Chuck Levinger, another very good friend, against a target of some importance. On the run, the enemy threw everything they had at the formation.

The drop was successful, the target covered with flames. But to get out of the valley, the flight had to fly very low along a corridor the enemy knew well. Hinson had just signaled Levinger thumbs-up, that the bombing run was excellent, when he took a direct hit, his left wing blew off, and his plane snapped twice and hit the ground in a ball of flame.

When Peter heard the news he was actively ill. He canceled his hotel reservation, returned to the base, picked up the new plane, and flew back to K-8.

There are many other tragic stories. Dale Christians roomed with Elmer Koski at Reese, where they both completed their aviation cadet training in the venerable T-6. The two were close friends. After graduation, Elmer was checked out in an F-51 and subsequently an F-84. One evening, Elmer was returning to base and prepared for a foul- weather landing. The 84 was still very new to him. Elmer missed his approach, stalled out, and was too low to correct. Dale lost a good friend that night and 52-Charlie added a name to its honor flight.

Bob Moon and John Smith were also good friends of Christians. Both men flew F-94s after graduation. Both were assigned to bases in Alaska. Moon lost his life while flying there and Smith was killed in an airplane accident shortly after completing his tour in 94s.

The power of friendship: It makes a mockery of death and grief becomes a subject for *Saturday Night Live*. When a friend is killed there is a moment of profound sadness— that moment passes, and in its wake are hours of laughter and stories and fond, fond memories.

FUJIGMO!

It was late May and meetings were being held in Panmunjom. There was talk of peace. But the war went on, the bombing continued. Every time the UN negotiator thought they had arrived at a settlement agreeable to both parties, the North Koreans broke off the talks. They were soon continued, but new demands were made. The two parties agreed on the 38th parallel as the line between North and South Korea. One of the terms of the peace was that any aircraft on the ground in North Korea when the war ended could remain in North Korea, but new aircraft could not be flown in.

As a result, in the later stages of the war our missions changed from strategic to tactical. Instead of carrying 500-pound bombs, we carried 100-pound bombs, two hundred of them, which we dropped on North Korean air bases. Our objective: to keep the North Koreans from flying in a bunch of aircraft just before the armistice began.

It was flawed thinking. As soon as the war was over, they began ferrying in MiG fighters. Besides, even if every bomb from fifteen B-29s hit the runway, two thousand Koreans with shovels had filled the holes before we reached Okinawa on our return.

On June 27, 1953, I completed my twenty-seventh combat mission. Captain Holmes let me take off and land our 29 that day. He even asked me to taxi it to the hard stand and shut the engines down. He had a hunch this might be my final mission and he was the kind of officer who knew how important it would be for me to control all aspects of my last mission in Korea—just one of the reasons everyone on our crew enjoyed flying with him. Our commanding officer was waiting at the hard stand. As I shut off the engines, the nose-wheel hatch was thrown open and the commander yelled into the cockpit, "FUJIGMO! Gentlemen, you are FUJIGMO!"

The sweetest non-word ever uttered. I had flown my final mission. FUJIGMO! "Fuck You Joe I Got My Orders." We were going home. Twenty-seven combat missions. Twenty-seven trips over enemy territory. Twenty-seven times wondering if that night was the night your plane would get hit. Twenty-seven times wiping the sweat from your hands as you turned the aircraft over to the radar operator for the bombing run. Twenty-seven times feeling the plane lift lightly into the sky as twenty tons of bombs fell through your bomb bay.

Every member of the crew felt a great sense of relief—and a touch of sadness because this would be our last mission together. Since Captain Holmes had taken over from Captain Smith our crew had become one. We were no longer officers or noncoms. We were a team who respected every other member of that team. We were friends, and we were a very proud group of young men.

FUJIGMO! Your tour is up and you will be shipping home. It's time to break out the champagne.

Lieutenants Lushbaugh, Winstead, Addison, McGowan, all from 52-C completed #100 on May 17, 1953. They're going home and seem pretty happy about it.

Fighter pilots had to fly 100 combat missions before they were FUJIGMO. B-29 pilots were released after 25 or so. An F-86 or F-84 pilot could fly a combat mission in two hours or less and often flew more than one mission a day. A B-29 pilot could fly only one mission every three days and each mission lasted twelve hours in the air and another twelve preparing for it.

But when that magic number was realized, there were smiles everywhere.

On June 27, 1952, I was awarded the Air Medal by my CO. Everything I was taught at Greenville and Enid and Randolph and Stead had made this day possible and brought me through some harrowing experiences, both physically dangerous and psychological. I look back on my five years in the service as five of the greatest years of my life and the six months in Okinawa as the best months I spent in the service.

The moment I was told my tour was up I began to miss it. I spent the next ten days in Kadena wandering aimlessly around the base

Awards and decorations time. A very proud co-pilot gets the Air Medal in front of the B-29 he flew.

while waiting to catch a MATS aircraft back to the States. Steve Walter, my bridge partner, had left the month before. Captain Holmes, who had flown only a dozen missions, was given a new crew. Others on my crew had shipped out to Tokyo. I was on one of the largest bases in the Far East and I was lonely.

Each evening I would walk to the flight line and watch the crews prepare for their mission. I wished them well, and I also wished I was going with them.

The long flight home began aboard a DC-4. Christmas was returned to me when I re-crossed the International Date Line on the flight to Hickam AFB in Hawaii. But Christmas in June isn't quite like Christmas in December. The only thing I opened that day was a bottle of scotch.

Wildman's crew checks each other's chutes.

Sherman's crew at parade rest.

The black-bellied 29 gets set for a night raid.

The crew listens to the boss.

Captain Lappo's crew all smiles.

Chutes are all lined up for inspection.

The MATS plane waited to take a lot of combat veterans back to the States.

While the accommodations weren't first class, there was a stewardess.

Finally, a Few Trash Haulers

A very young Joe Beck just got his wings and bars. He would fly 29s in Korea and retire a colonel in the reserve.

Not all members of 52-Charlie flew jets; many of us, like Joe Beck, were multi-engine pilots, affectionately called "trash haulers." Beck trained in B-25s at Vance and B-29s at Randolph before being posted to Okinawa to fly the 29 in combat.

On each of his first three combat missions, a 29 was lost. Joe did the arithmetic; there were thirty planes in his group and he was scheduled to fly thirty combat missions. That did not bode will.

On his third mission, Beck watched a 29 take a hit. He was on the command set with the co-pilot as the young man prepared to bail out. Beck wished him luck. Forty years later, at a B-29 reunion in Seattle, he met the co-pilot and the two had a wonderful chat.

Beck was one hell of a pilot but not a particularly good mathematician. For years he maintained he had flown 29 combat missions, but recently he checked his log and found he really had flown only 25. On one mission, his bomb bay doors froze in the open position just after he had dropped his bombs. Major Davis, his Airplane Commander, ordered Beck to try to crank the doors down. That meant he had to go into the bomb bay, strap himself to a bomb rack, look down 25,000 feet to the frozen ground below, and try his best to crank the damn doors shut.

The doors didn't budge.

Open bomb bay doors create drag, so much so that they could not make it back to Okinawa. They flew instead to Itazuke, where they fixed the problem, had a warm breakfast, and took off for Kadena.

Harold Cobb is a veteran of three wars. He enlisted May 17, 1943, at the age of seventeen and was assigned to maintenance duties, repairing P-40s and P-51s. In 1951 Cobb applied for aviation cadets and was accepted. He flew T-6s, B-25s, and the B-29.

Cobb spent the next few years at Barksdale with an occasional TDY trip. During one of these trips, he was about halfway to the Azores from Bermuda when all hell broke loose. He lost two engines. It was vital to reduce weight and the most obvious answer was to jettison the rear bomb bay tank. It half-worked. The shackles on one side of the tank released, but those on the other side did not. This could have been fatal if the tank was allowed to dangle in the slipstream. Fortunately, the reticent shackles released, and the fuel tank fell free. They were able to close the bomb bay doors and return safely to Bermuda.

Before retiring, Cobb served in the Vietnam War as commander of the Allied 14th Contract Maintenance Unit. After twenty years of service in three different wars, Harold Cobb retired with the rank of lieutenant colonel.

Another B-29 junkie, Jerry Michaletz, made the right decision after primary and chose multi-engine school. After checking out in the B-29 at Randolph he was sent to Yakota, Japan, to fly combat.

Michaletz had an engine shot out in an early mission and had to land at K-13. He was also forced to make an emergency landing at Itazuke after a second engine acted up. But Jerry's real problem wasn't engine failure, it was running on empty. On a training flight, the bomb bay fuel transfer pump failed and he was unable to transfer fuel from the bomb bay tank to the wing tanks. When Michaletz put his 29 down, there was zero— that's zero—gallons of usable fuel in his tanks. Dry as the desert.

Another time, he landed a C-45 with only five gallons of gas left. When Michaletz retired from the service he purchased a light aircraft. If he were ever to ask me to fly with him, I would damn sure bring along my Texaco credit card.

Jerry Michaletz and one of the few times he had sufficient fuel.

Bill Payne also flew B-29s in the Korean War. He was stationed at Kadena in Okinawa. Payne's most exciting mission occurred one night when flak exploded under his right wing, lifted the huge aircraft up, and turned it over on its side. The A/C recovered quickly, but not without a moment of reflection. Bill and his A/C decided at that moment they would no longer wait for the photo flash bomb to hit before turning the plane off the target. They brought no strike photos back that night, only some memories they didn't relish.

Bill Payne, second from the left in the front row.

Bill Payne had an excellent crew and they distinguished themselves. So much so that every man on the crew was awarded a Bronze Star, and Payne has the pictures to prove it. Problem: No one seems to have the paperwork. And despite the fact that Bill has searched every Air Force archive and contacted all the members of his crew, the paper is still missing. When Bill retired from the Air Force he attended law school, and he is a practicing attorney today.

Not every military aircraft is designed for combat, nor is every soldier, sailor, or airman sent to the front lines. Still, these men risked their lives on a daily basis to make sure that those flying combat had the best possible chance of returning to their families after their tour of duty. They were participants at the highest level and this book would not be complete if they were not acknowledged.

Diddle, Doran, Dombaugh, and Griffith all completed their training in B-29s at Randolph and were then sent either to tanker school at West Palm Beach or Barksdale AFB in Louisiana.

Diddle, Griffith, Dombaugh, and Doran, all retired tanker pilots.

It takes precision flying to transfer fuel from a tanker to a jet while bobbing up and down in the thin air at 20,000 feet. Flying tankers during a war is one of the most critical jobs there is. Missions are planned around the tanker. If a fuel transfer is not successfully completed lives could be lost, planes could fall into the sea. The tanker pilot had to fly in good weather and bad.

The KB-97, America's flying gas station.

Jim Diddle flew a 97 out of Anchorage, Alaska, where the weather is both unpredictable and dangerous. One day Diddle's squadron was scheduled to fly a refueling mission several hundred miles south of the base. The weather conditions were intolerable, but there were three fuel-starved B-47s waiting for Diddle's squadron. They could not abort that day.

Diddle's was the third plane to take off. The runway ended at a cliff some three hundred feet above the water. As his plane climbed out over the cliff it became virtually uncontrollable, due to extreme low-level turbulence. Even with power adjustments and full aileron and rudder deflections, the wings could not be controlled. Jim Diddle was certain he was about to crash into the sea when a gust of wind lifted his plane to a manageable altitude.

Diddle was thankful he was leaving the weather at Anchorage. He set course south to his destination, sat back in his seat, and took a deep breath, all too soon. His windscreen shattered and he was going to have to return to his base and land in that frightening weather.

His landing was the equal of his takeoff. If anything, the turbulence had increased. There were lateral shifts, wind shears, everything imaginable. Diddle put his gear down but immediately retracted it because of the extreme side-to-side gyrations of the aircraft. Just then he was told there was smoke coming from one of his engines. He

Jim Diddle arrives home after a TDY to greet his wife and child. The brass was there to meet him.

could not shut it down; he needed it. Just as he leveled off for landing, he dropped the gear. Three greens and a safe landing followed. The engine fire was put out and Diddle made his way to the officers' club for a few shots of Jack Daniel's.

Diddle was lucky. Another member of 52-Charlie was not. Bob Moon—en route to Korea in a C-124, crashed on landing in foul weather at Anchorage. Moon and all the passengers aboard the plane were killed. Diddle was a career officer and retired a full colonel, with no desire to vacation in Alaska.

Jim Griffith also ended up in KB-97s along with another classmate, Paul Fisher. Griffith refueled aircraft from bases in Morocco, Europe, Bermuda, England, and the United States. He had the distinction of literally helping to save Holland. In 1953, the Netherlands suffered through the worst storm of the century. The dikes at the Zuider Zee were breached and Holland was about to be overrun by the North Sea. It is interesting that when tragedy hits, America is usually the first to respond. And so it was in 1953.

Griffith and his group of tankers supported the drop of thousands upon thousands of sand bags, used to hold back the sea. These bags had to be dropped at a very low altitude, which took precision flying and a lot of guts.

Some years later Griffith was visiting Holland and told the story of the sand bags. From that moment on virtually everything was on the house. Jim Griffith retired from the Air Force in 1955 and joined the reserve, advancing in rank to lieutenant colonel.

Bird's-eye view of a B-47 being refueled.

Ray Dombaugh flew KC-97 tankers during his entire Air Force career and got so caught up in the gas business that when he retired after four years, he became a geologist and made a small fortune in oil.

Doran spent the rest of his air force career in Salina, Kansas, flying the 97 and refueling B-47s. Salina was a dry community at that time, which prompted Doran to leave the service as soon as he could. By the time he got out he had accumulated 2200 flying hours.

The tanker pilot could say only yes. He flew when he was told to fly regardless of the conditions. That took skilled pilots, pilots like Doran, Diddle, Dombaugh, and Griffith, pilots trained in the class of 52-Charlie.

Part Three

The Vietnam War

The Vietnam War was the longest and most divisive conflict in the history of the United States. It began in 1959 and was not settled until 1975. Between four to six million people were killed; 58,000 Americans were lost, 304,000 were wounded. 52-Charlie was there. Bill Pearce, Larry Gardner, and Boque Harrison were all awarded the Silver Star for gallantry under fire during their tour of duty in Vietnam.

Back for Seconds

This picture of Bill Pearce is obviously damaged, But nothing compared to some of the planes he flew.

Bill Pearce flew in three wars. In WW II he flew twenty-three combat missions as a navigator. After graduating from cadets, he flew 107 combat missions in Korea, including the one in which he interrupted a lovers' tryst. He followed that with another 223 combat missions in Vietnam, where he often returned to base with his A-1 Skyraider so full of holes it was a wonder it stayed in the air.

I asked Bill which mission in Vietnam he considered his most dramatic.

"That's easy. It was the time I escorted two Air America helicopters up to the China border. The purpose of this clandestine mission was to insert a dozen or so special OPS troops along the Ho Chi Minh

Trail. They spoke Vietnamese and carried radios, curved knives, Burb guns, and piano wire for silent assassinations. They dressed in black and looked like they were reading for the part of Rambo. They were there to cause as much havoc as they could, take out a few leaders, and report on the activity along the trail.

"Flying my wing was a recent graduate of the USAF academy who had flown only a couple of missions. I instructed the Huey pilots not to change channels without my permission and to take all instructions from me. Unfortunately, I failed to tell my wingman that."

"I have a feeling...."

"You're right, Ted. The mission got a bit spotty. The Trail is quite wide in places and before I could tell them to land on the east side of the Trail, my wingman ordered the Hueys to land on the west side. When they did, all hell broke loose because they set their 'copters down in the middle of a North Vietnamese Army rest camp. A firefight began the likes of which I had never seen before. My wingman dropped a napalm canister on the left side of the Hueys and I dropped one on the right side. It scared the hell out of the troops in the 'copters but it also slowed the enemy down for a few minutes. In the next forty-five minutes, we dropped our other two napalm canisters, fired every single round of ammunition we had and all twenty of our rockets."

"Did the Hueys get out?"

"Yeah, yeah, they did, but some of the soldiers were killed. When I got back to my base I counted 139 holes in my plane. God knows why I wasn't hit or why a critical system in my A-1 wasn't destroyed. By the way, I was awarded the Silver Star for that mission."

"Congratulations. Any other good things happen to you while you were in Vietnam?"

"To be sure! I was flying at night, being guided by an AWAC radar plane. Our mission was to monitor the Trail. The Vietnamese were bringing in heavy guns to support the TET offensive. They directed me to a suspicious blip and just as I was preparing for a run, I saw an orange ball of fire heading my way that was anything but friendly. I felt one hell of a jolt and I knew I was hit. I broke off and reported to the AWAC, who asked if I wanted to return to base. I told them I would like to make a run at that gun before going home but I wanted to come in from a different direction. They set it up and I launched a few rockets, hit the gun, and took off for my base. That gun was Russian and it was the first radar-controlled 20 mm weapon we had seen."

"What was your damage?'

"I had a two-and-a-half foot hole in my stabilizer. That's a big hole. Again, I was lucky it did not hit any control cables."

I suppose when you fly 223 combat missions, you will get hit once in a while. Bill Pearce finally retired after fighting in three wars. He had earned a moment's rest.

Yes, Virginia, There Really Is a Stork

George Smith flew 51s with Don Monchil in Korea long before he became a famous babysitter.

Most have seen the terrible pictures of the last days of Saigon before the North Vietnamese took control of the city. The last flights out were filled with young and old alike, but there were many who had to be left behind.

That's the picture that stays with us. What most people do not know is that those were not the last rescue flights into Saigon.

George Smith, a member of 52-Charlie, was a pilot on that last rescue flight and it happened three days after Saigon fell.

George was a radio operator in the Army Air Corp at the end of WW II when he was discharged. He enjoyed flying so when the Korea war began George re-enlisted and was assigned to 52-Charlie, graduating from Craig AFB and gunnery school at Luke. During the Korean fracas he was stationed in Tokyo, flying the Mustang. After Korea he retired from the Air Force and joined Pan American Airlines, where he continued to fly for the next twenty-five years.

George Smith at the 38th parallel in Korea, the most famous line ever drawn in the sand.

Many of his flights were charter into Vietnam. Smith delivered the first "advisors" in 1960. They were being flown in as tourists but Smith knew better. They had army haircuts; they were young, and carried themselves with military discipline. They were not there to visit shrines and enjoy South Vietnamese hospitality.

Smith continued to deliver men and materials throughout the Vietnam War and often came under fire. Bullet holes in engine nacelles were common. He flew almost every aircraft from the 377 double bubble to the 747.

He was flying over Saigon the night the city fell. He watched as the skies filled with fireworks, the biggest display of its kind he had ever seen. When he landed he learned the fate of Saigon and assumed that would be his last flight there. But that was not to be the case.

A few days later he was told he had one more flight to make. President Ford had ordered two 747s into Saigon to pick up babies and their nurses. This mission was so secret it was not covered by paperwork. Voice orders only.

The North Vietnamese had agreed they would not attack the planes if they carried no ordnance. Three days after Saigon fell, Smith piloted a special 747 from Washington and landed in Saigon. In the bushes surrounding the airfield were enemy tanks and soldiers. Smith knew they were there. The two planes landed and one pilot from each plane got off to meet with a representative of the North Vietnamese. The two command pilots, including Smith, remained on their aircrafts with orders that if the enemy initiated any action, they were to take off immediately, leaving the other pilots behind.

The two 747s filled their planes with babies. There were babies in the seats, babies under the seats, babies in the john, everywhere babies. Smith estimated that his 747 alone carried more than a thousand babies and a hundred or more nurses. He flew to Tokyo, where he departed the plane before it continued on to Seattle and Washington.

George Smith did almost everything one could do in the service and managed to deliver more babies in one night than an obstetrician could deliver in a lifetime.

Fair Winds

Warren Henderson twenty-five years after his graduation. Now a colonel with a plethora of heroic tales to tell that all began with a favoring wind

Sailors dream of fair winds and a safe journey. Pilots have been known to share that same dream.

Warren Henderson flew in Korea and in Vietnam. In both theaters of operation he was shot down. In both instances he managed to get back to friendly territory.

In Korea, Henderson flew F-84s and on his fiftieth mission he was hit by ground fire. His 84 was mortally wounded and he knew he would have to bail out. The question was when and where. Henderson prayed that his stricken aircraft could fly the few miles back to South Korea, but his engine quit. Then the gods took over and the winds blew Warren's crippled aircraft back to our side of the line so that when he bailed out he landed in a forward army mess center rather than in enemy territory.

Henderson flew two tours in Vietnam. During his first tour as an air liaison officer, he flew 262 combat missions in the L-19 and survived without ever sustaining serious combat damage. This is remarkable considering the vulnerability of the plane he flew. In his second tour, he was made commander of an F-100 squadron at Phan Rang and given the rank of light colonel.

Here Henderson was up to his old tricks, but this time without the benefit of a fair breeze. One morning as he completed his drop, he was hit by ground fire. And his F-100 caught fire. His plane was terminal and he knew it. It was only a matter of time before he would have to bail out.

Henderson's wingman watched his leader's F-100 go down, powerless to help, and when he returned to the base, he reported that Henderson's plane was on fire when it hit the ground. He also reported that he saw no chute. This report was sent to his wife, who was certain that she had lost her husband.

But the winds of chance were also blowing that day. Unbeknownst to his wingman, Henderson had bailed out over a jungle in Cambodia and landed in an area populated by the enemy, where the heat and humidity were intense. Henderson could not seek help, nor could he walk out. After three days in the steaming jungle with virtually no supplies, Henderson contacted a helicopter that happened over his position. He was picked up and returned to his base.

Two wars! Two nylon letdowns. Two planes lost. Henderson was becoming an ace but for the wrong side. He was rotated back to Clovis, New Mexico, where he would spend the rest of his military career as director of operations. He had had enough combat for a lifetime. Besides, the Air Force was running out of planes.

When Henderson retired in 1977 he purchased a fleet of aircraft and ran charters, air taxies, and an air ambulance service for the next twenty years.

As a registered nurse his wife, Lyn, helped out on medical flights. She was more than a nurse; she was a grief counselor. She spent time at Oklahoma City following the bombing there and at Ground Zero following the 9/11 attack. She also helped manage an emergency clinic in Perrine, Florida, to tend to victims of Hurricane Andrew.

Oh, we mustn't forget Warren L. Henderson, their son. He graduated from the Air Force Academy and reached the rank of a bird colonel. At one point in his career, young Warren Henderson was assigned as the senior executive officer for the Under Secretary of the Air Force, Peter B. Teets.

Quite a family!

Warren senior passed away in 2000. Were he here today, Warren junior said with a smile, he would insist his father salute him.

Like father, like son, like mother, a very dedicated family of overachievers.

Warren's family will long remember that he was one hell of a pilot; a proud member of 52-Charlie, and at one critical stage in his life was carried to safety in the arms of a gentle breeze.

Forward Air Controller—Combat at Its Most Dangerous

The only gun Bo Harrison had on his aircraft was what he carried aboard. These forward air controllers flew low, flew slow, and had no way to protect themselves except their own skill. That is why so many of Bo's fellow pilots were shot down.

Boque Harrison spent a lifetime in the air and most of that was behind enemy lines. Four hundred and fifty missions! He flew in Korea. He flew in Vietnam. He had a lifetime of memories and a chest full of ribbons.

After graduation from cadets, Harrison was posted to K-13 in Korea, where he flew cover for the B-29s in an F-94. Harrison reported his tour in Korea was uneventful.

It was not so fourteen years later when he flew 435 missions in 328 days in Vietnam.

Harrison was a forward air controller, flying the Cessna O1E, a plane with a top speed of 180 knots. That isn't fast enough to win the Indianapolis 500. He was often required to fly his plane so low that David could have knocked it out of the sky with his slingshot. Its fuselage was one-sixteenth of an inch thick and the weaponry consisted of eight white phosphorous marking rockets, an M-16 rifle which Harrison carried aboard with three clips, a bunch of different-color smoke cans, and some wonderfully ingenious grenades that fit snuggly into a mess hall glass.

The Viet Cong knew that the Cessna carried no weapons and they'd often thumb their noses at the FAC pilots as they flew overhead. Harrison didn't exactly appreciate that, so he came up with an answer. A grenade in a glass. He would either pull the pin from the grenade or break the glass against the side of the plane and toss it out. The grenade would blow up a few feet above the soldiers. Good-bye soldiers.

This small plane with its fixed landing gear, stubby wings, and 100-hp engine was one of the most important combat planes in Vietnam. It was a spotter aircraft, yet not nearly as fast or as well protected as the T-6. More than 200 FAC pilots never returned. Hundreds others were shot down and rescued. Flying forward air control was one of the most dangerous assignments in Vietnam.

Harrison's wing after a mission. Shell holes were the rule, not the exception. Bo flew more than 400 missions in less than a year.

Harrison's responsibility was to ferret out the enemy, whether they were on a path, in trees, waiting in ambush, hidden in caves, or ambling down the Ho Chi Minh Trail. And once he found them, he would spot them with a flare and direct F-100s or F-4Cs to the target. Because he flew so low and so slowly, he often returned to his base with holes in his wings and his fuselage.

Boque Harrison was a modest, quiet man whom I had the pleasure of meeting on the phone shortly before he died of cancer. This remarkable pilot told me several stories about his participation in the Vietnam War. He was awarded the Silver Star for the mission he flew on May 26, 1967. This is how he described that mission.

"I was sent to support the ground operations of the 2d Battalion, 14th Infantry, 25th Infantry Division, against a Viet Cong force that was well dug in and camouflaged. In the first twenty minutes of contact the 2nd Battalion had taken twelve dead and twenty wounded. They were hopelessly pinned down. I had two flights of F-100s and I started putting them in. They dropped 500-pounders and napalms and sprayed them with 50 mm shells. I marked VC targets on seven different passes and each time I took several rounds of ground fire. I controlled thirty separate ground strikes by F-100s, which kept the VC pinned down.

"However, as our troops began to air-evac their dead and wounded the enemy opened fire on them. I went in low to divert some of their fire and about then their battalion C/O called me and said he had taken hits and had to retire.

"'You have my command,' he said, 'treat it fairly.'

"I almost choked. An Air Force FAC in command of a ground battalion! It just doesn't happen.

"During the next three hours I stayed on the deck directing fire on the VC positions. Just then Charlie Company came under heavy fire and sent out six scouts to locate the Cong. I watched as all six were cut down in seconds. I could see the VC in the trees and bunkers from which they were firing.

"'I'll mark their positions. You fire at my smoke, okay?'"

"'Anything, for God's sakes, anything!' was their response.

"I had four smoke cans between my legs. I approached their position below treetop level and as I popped up over the trees, I dropped the smoke cans. I repeated the procedure two more times. It worked. They stopped firing and within minutes they had dispersed. Charlie Company got out without any further losses.

"Later at my BOQ, a couple of GIs, one with a full upper-body cast and the other with a bandaged head, came up to me, saluted, and thanked me for saving their lives."

One of the planes in which Harrison flew four hundred missions in less than a year. He spent more time in the air than he did on the ground. Being shot at!

Major Harrison flew several other missions, equally hazardous, equally heroic. It was not rare for him to fly more than sixteen hours against a single target, landing only to refuel. He even flew the mission depicted in Oliver Stone's movie, *Platoon.* Harrison told me the movie was quite accurate except for one thing. The troops never asked to have bombs dropped on their position.

The ground war in Vietnam was hell. The air war was almost as bad and Harrison landed his plane time and time again with holes punched through the wings and the fuselage. Still he was lucky. He was never wounded.

Strange things happen at ten thousand feet in a plane the size of a 01E when you have one hand on the stick and you are holding a pair of binoculars with the other. When Bo told me the following story, I found it difficult to believe. But he swore it was true.

"I was flying over an area which a B-52 had recently carpet bombed with its load of 500-pounders. It had been a hot spot, loaded with enemy troops and equipment. The B-52 changed all that. Following the bombing, it appeared to be nothing more than an uninhabited piece of desolate terrain. But I saw something. And I betcha, Ted, you can't guess what I saw."

"Enemy soldiers? A Jeep? I give up."

"I saw footprints!"

"From ten thousand feet? C'mon, Bo. I'll swallow almost anything, but footprints from ten thousand feet? That's a stretch."

"Stretch it may be, but that's what I saw with my binoculars. Ted, fine powder-like sand spreads across much of Vietnam, sand so soft it would retain footprints. When the sun is at a precise angle, shadows are created. And even something as small as a footprint would leave a shadow. Where there are footprints there are people. So for the next two to three days, I continued to check the area. The footprints were multiplying and they followed a trail that disappeared into a group of trees large enough to hide trucks, army personnel, and ordnance.

"The next day, I saw something new. A black object darted out of the trees on to the trail and then back. It happened several times and each time it was accompanied by a puff of dirt. It didn't take long before I realized what it was. The black object was a dog. The puff of dirt was a stick being thrown by the dog's master."

"All of this from 10,000 feet?"

"You bet. Anyhow, that was all the proof I needed. I checked with control and was told that there were two F-100s in my area that were looking for a target of opportunity. I gave them that opportunity. They asked me to spot the target with a flare, but I didn't want to alert the enemy. I asked them to hold at altitude until they could see the footprints and when they had done so to drop down and release their bombs in trail from where the footprints began into the trees. The F-100s did exactly as suggested. The hiding place was demolished. Later a group of American soldiers visited the area and found over a hundred casualties, an ammunition dump, and lots and lots of destroyed military equipment."

Bo Harrison had one adventure after another throughout his long and distinguished military career. He retired a bird colonel, a widely respected pilot, and an honored member of 52-Charlie, with eyes that could still see footprints from 10,000 feet in the air. During his career, Bo won the Silver Star, a Distinguished Flying Cross with an oak leaf cluster and enough ribbons to open an arts and craft shop.

A Long Way to Go to Meet a Future Senator

Colonel Carl Crumpler in a F4D had a date with destiny which began on July 5, 1968. It would last almost five years.

Warren Henderson and Carl Crumpler had a lot in common. Both retired from the service as colonels. Both flew combat in Vietnam and both were shot down. Crumpler graduated from Greenville and went to Vance for multi-engine training but switched to fighters when the opportunity arose.

He checked out in jets and was assigned to Eddie Rickenbacker's famous '"Hat-in-the-Ring" squadron, flying F-86s and Ds. He was such a fine pilot that he was transferred to North American Aviation to fly production tests on F-86 Ds and Fs. He spent nine months in this program.

Crumpler was on a fast track. The military sent him to Okinawa for two years and then on a series of special assignments to Selfridge, Tyndall, and Amarillo Air Force Bases and ultimately to Iran as aircraft maintenance advisor to the Shah's Imperial Iranian Air Force. In 1968, as a lieutenant colonel, Crumpler was posted to the 8th Tactical Fighter wing at Ubon, Thailand, to fly combat in Vietnam. On the afternoon of July fifth he, with his backseat pilot/radar observer, Lt. Mike Burns, flew his forty-fourth combat mission in a two-plane formation about sixty miles north of the DMZ. Crumpler spotted something suspicious on the ground. He rolled in and dropped his bombs on a revetment, leveling off at about 8000 feet.

He felt three bumps. Thump! Thump! Thump! Three 37 mm shells had hit his plane. His fire warning-light blazed. He shut down the starboard engine and began a climb. He knew he could not make it back to the base. His only option was to fly out to sea and bail out there. Carl leveled off at 15,000 feet and set a course for the ocean, his plane a torch, trailing fire. Suddenly, he lost control. The plane went into a spin and dove towards the ground.

Crumpler and Burns had no option—they were forced to bail out. Crumpler landed in an area bristling with soldiers and gun emplacements. He hid in a bush and watched as soldiers walked back and forth in front of his hiding place. The soldiers finally moved off and he breathed a heavy sigh of relief. Then, one soldier stopped, looked down at the ground, turned and walked directly to where he was hiding. He thrust a rifle into the bush and Crumpler was captured. GI issue was the villain. The boots worn by pilots had small cleats, which left a distinctive pattern in the dirt. The soldier noticed the marks and walked to where they led.

Crumpler's elbows were tied behind his back and a noose was put around his neck. A Vietnamese soldier hit him with his rifle butt, knocking him to the ground.

The soldier pulled him to his feet and marched him into a small town, where fifty or so women and children beat him with sticks and stones as he passed.

"They beat the crap out of me!" he reported.

The guards could not control the civilians and were concerned for their own safety. With a sharp tug on the rope around his neck, the soldiers forced Crumpler to run, which probably saved his life. They outran the townspeople.

That night they stuffed Crumpler into a small chicken coop. A short time later the coop was reopened and Mike Burns was thrown in. Later that night, the guards led their two prisoners through a series of slit trenches to a small school building, where they were told to lie on some benches and sleep. Needless to say, they did not sleep.

They spent the next day walking some three miles, bound and without shoes, across the dry terrain to a meeting room in a small village. It was a unique room, built six feet below the surface of the ground with tunnels carved in each corner. In the event of an air raid, the occupants of the room would hide in these tunnels.

Crumpler and Burns remained here for the next eight days; drinking boiled water so hot the cup burned their hands and eating fish heads and rice. The guards were civil and maintained control, but the civilians hated the Americans and attacked them at every opportunity. The women were far more hostile than the men.

Major Gobel James, an F-105 pilot who had been shot down, joined the two men in the room. When James had bailed out at about six hundred knots, his leg was separated at the knee and dangled as if held by rubber bands. The guards fashioned a bamboo splint, but James was in terrible pain.

Crumpler told me, "Gobel is one of the toughest men I ever met."

James lay in one of the tunnels for hours, his face inches from the top of the tunnel. When they finally moved, Crumpler and Burns carried the major on a board and tightened the makeshift splint when needed.

The prisoners were then trucked to Hanoi over the most violent terrain imaginable. Jungles, mountains, potholes, boulders, everything. It was brutal.

The first night, they stayed in a truck park with hundreds of other trucks. They came under an air attack and everyone ran for their lives. Cluster bombs were being dropped and had a single bomb hit the target, Crumpler and his friends would most likely have been killed, as the explosions would have been exponential.

On the way north, the prisoners were often hassled by the locals. One rabid young man pulled a pistol from his leather holster and aimed it at Crumpler's head, screaming at the top of his lungs.

"The barrel of the gun was a foot wide, or so it seemed," Crumpler told me.

The guards yelled at the young man and chased him off. On reflection, Crumpler wonders if that scene had not been staged.

Two weeks later they finally arrived at their destination, Hoa Lo Prison, better known to the POWs as the Hanoi Hilton. On arrival, most of the POWs were held in an interrogation section of the prison, which they nicknamed "Heartbreak Hotel."

Interrogation and pain continued for the POWs.

Three to four days later, Crumpler was moved once again to another area the prisoners affectionately called Las Vegas. It was a cellblock for high-ranking officers, commanders, lieutenant colonels, and above.

Crumpler spent the next sixteen months in solitary confinement in a cellblock called Star Dust. He was not allowed to lie down in his seven-by-seven cell during the day. He was told he was a criminal of the worst kind and he should reflect on that, sitting up with nothing to divert his attention. Boredom was his most-feared captor. If a POW was caught talking with another prisoner he was beaten.

Crumpler said, however, "You can't keep an American from talking. We communicated daily by means of a 25-matrix box called a 'tap code' that contained all but one letter in the alphabet. We would tap messages on the walls, using letter codes, and always received a response. The walls of Las Vegas often sounded as though a hundred woodpeckers were hard at work." During the weekends the guards were few and conversations between prisoners were extensive.

Once a day Crumpler was taken out of his cell for thirty minutes to a cement sink where he washed, and once a month water was thrown on the floor of his cell and swept into one of many floor drains, the home of the rats that infested Las Vegas.

Interrogation slackened off. At first it was once a day, then once a week, and finally maybe once a month. If the North Vietnamese were certain a prisoner had no other information of value, the beatings were discontinued.

One day, however, Crumpler was taken to interrogation where the Vietnamese officer spoke perfect English.

"I knew that was serious."

The interrogator was looking for information about the odd-looking pods under the wings of a fighter. These pods were electronic countermeasure devices that interfered with SAM missiles. Once launched, the missile went ballistic because of these pods. Crumpler was certain the Russians wanted information about them. He lied his way through the session. He was becoming very good at that.

His sixteen months of solitary confinement ended about the time that Ho Chi Minh died. The Vietnamese adored the man, accepting him as a god, a king, a spiritual leader. When he died, North Vietnam went into shock and things began to change. There was a feeling that the POWs had value as bargaining chips, and their treatment improved.

The Vietnamese moved Crumpler into a second cellblock where he was imprisoned with two naval aviators, Byron Fuller, who would later reach the rank of rear admiral, and Ken Coskey, a Navy A6 squadron commander. For the first time in almost two years, Carl had someone to talk to, someone to hope with.

As prisoners were added to the Hilton, one of the first things they did was to surreptitiously introduce themselves to their fellow inmates. Crumpler was completing his exercises one morning in the prison yard when a prisoner whispered to him from a nearby window. The prisoner had just been transferred to the Hilton. That day Carl Crumpler met John McCain, by voice only. Their wives knew each other from Florida where their children grew up together, yet Crumpler had never met the future senator.

There were seven large rooms at the Hilton. McCain and Crumpler were moved into room seven along with forty-four other ranking officers. George "Bud" Day was there. Bud was the most highly decorated American since Audie Murphy. He was later awarded the Congressional Medal of Honor. Jim Stockdale was a roommate and also a Medal of Honor recipient. Jerry Denton, future senator from Alabama, was one of the forty-six. These men would spend the next eighty-three days together playing bridge and chess and reminiscing about better times.

One Sunday the room seven prisoners decided to hold church. This infuriated the guards, who insisted that services be discontinued. Tell that to an American. The next two Sundays services were held. The guards took one of the leaders outside for punishment. All the members of seven began singing the national anthem at the top of their lungs. Soon room six joined in, then five, and so on. That was it. The Vietnamese had had enough. The prisoners were reassigned two men to a cell and Crumpler never saw McCain again until they were repatriated on March 14, 1973. Gobel James was repatriated about the same time. Crumpler spent four years, eight months, and twenty-one days as a POW. The most exciting and vivid memory he has was when Nixon countermanded former President Johnson's standing order and released the B-52s to bomb North Vietnam. They began their missions a week before Christmas of 1972. It was then Crumpler and his fellow prisoners knew there would soon be a prisoner exchange. And there was. The war actually did not end until 1975, but hostilities in the north were discontinued.

Carl Crumpler and his lovely wife Jane live in Florida. His fellow POW resides in Arizona but spends most of his time in Washington. They both served their country well and are very proud of it.

There are thousands of Crumpler's and there are thousands of McCain's and aren't we lucky for that!

John McCain being captured by Vietnamese civilians.
Carl Crumpler gets a roommate.

Part Four

Unspoken Heroes of the Class of 52-Charlie

52-Charlie is a proud group. We've had more than our share of heroes, of outstanding pilots and remarkable leaders. One of these leaders was stationed in Vietnam but because of his rank was not allowed to fly combat. Another had experiences in three different wars and had a huge impact on the Air Force and its people. A third watched as his plane and his crew were shot down in WW II. A fourth won the Strategic Air Command's most prestigious award for excellence in the air. I would be remiss if I didn't tell their stories.

Star Power

Major General Don Bennett, the highest-ranking officer in the class of 52-Charlie.

52-Charlie graduated 420 cadets, all officers. The odds that one or two might reach the rank of general were fair. However, in the mix of that 420 were cadets like McDonnell, Griffith, Gushee, Doran, Fausel, etc., so that decreased the odds considerably. The Greenville Crazies were not destined to become shoulder heavy. But there was one Greenville Crazy who broke the rules and ended up with a pair of stars on his shoulders.

Don Bennett.

Bennett entered Greenville as a student officer. Obviously he had a head start. After graduating from Greenville, Bennett was sent to Vance AFB to spend another six months in T-6s, thirteen months in all. By the time he got his wings, he was eager to fly something that had a tricycle gear and a lot more speed. He got his wish. He checked out in the T-33 at Wichita, where he learned that flying aerobatics in a jet is one of the most exhilarating experiences a pilot can have.

Nellis AFB was next on the agenda, where Don learned to fire his guns while trying to keep his bird aloft.

The future general was on a fast track. He spent more time packing and unpacking than he did doing anything else except flying. From Nellis he went to Victorville to the 94th Fighter Intercept Squadron and his first Sabre jet, the F-86A. Moody and all-weather instrument training was next. Then Tyndal and the F-86D. Bennett was the first second lieutenant in the Air Force to fly this plane. It was reserved for more experienced pilots. However, Bennett's record as a young pilot was exceptional. It was a love affair at first takeoff. He and his 52-C partner, Carl Crumpler, went to the North American plant at Los Angeles on a TDY to fly production tests in the F-86D.

The future general prepares for a ride in the 86-D.

In 1955 Bennett was posted to Landstuhl Air Base in Germany. Three years later he was transferred to West Virginia and then to Westover AFB, Massachusetts. About the time he learned the names of the streets in Westover, it was time to pack his bags once again. This time to Andover, England, and the Royal Air Force staff college, followed by a posting to the RAF station at Coltishall, England, as a squadron commander.

This was the posting that Bennett enjoyed the most. The planes he flew there were English, including the Electric Lightning, perhaps the most advanced fighter of its time. Bennett considered the Lightning the finest plane he ever flew. Shortly after arriving in Coltishall, he was made an instructor pilot.

The Mach 2 RAF Lightning. It held the world speed record and was one of the finest aerobatic planes in service.

All good things come to an end and so too did his English experience. He returned to the States and was assigned to the 436th wing in Dover. Even that did not last long. From Dover Bennett went to Scott AFB and then on to Vietnam as an advisor to the Vietnamese Air Force. Bennett had an itch to fly combat, but because of his rank, or perhaps his security clearance, he was not allowed to fly over enemy territory.

A man with the experience of Maj. Gen. Don Bennett has stories to tell, moments to remember, moments to forget. One of those moments occurred when, as the test pilot of his squadron, he drew the short straw during the evacuation of a base. He was given the least airworthy bird to fly. Its leading edges were being held together by duct tape. A pilot had flown that plane into the tow-target cable, virtually destroying the leading edge of the wing and stabilizer. In addition, the forward fire-warning light was on constantly. Bennett made it to his destination without incident, but he had a few thoughts during the flight. The plane was redlined after Bennett landed it safely.

Another moment, one to forget. While in the RAF, he was training a pilot for an aerobatic mission. The young pilot was a cocky kid. Bennett trailed the young man in a Hawker Hunter, screaming directions most of the time. But the cocky kid knew better. He broke altitude barriers and flew his plane to the edge of disaster. After they landed, Bennett gave the kid an earful.

Unfortunately, none of it sank in. The next day, the pilot killed himself doing exactly what Don had told him not to do.

Two stars and a host of stories to tell. Seven thousand hours in the air in every conceivable type of aircraft. Wing commander responsible for thousands of young people and the direction of one of America's foremost strike forces. That's a load to put on one man's shoulders, but that's also why they place two stars there.

Bennett retired after thirty-five years in the military. And then he really got busy. He was appointed director of airports for the city of St Louis at Lambert International Airport. He was active with the Air Force Association and with the American Association of Airport Executives. He was a member of the St. Louis Rotary Club. He served as the police commissioner of O'Fallon, Illinois, and a member of the planning authority for the greater St. Louis metropolitan area. If Missouri or Illinois could have given Bennett his third star, they would have done so in a heartbeat.

Don Bennett, a proud member of 52-Charlie and not a bad pilot, either, with enough stories to keep his grandchildren riding a knee for hours at a time.

Don Bennett, third from the left, discusses the formation aerobatic mission just flown with Lieutenant Colonel Rabel and Captains Harris and Lawless. Pilots and Italians talk with their hands.

Colonel Everything

Colonel Howard Pierson. Check the ribbons. If it was done Howie probably did it.

Howard Pierson began his military career as a seventeen-year-old sailor aboard the *USS Iowa* during WW II before joining the Air Force. He saw action in the seas off Okinawa under attack by the Japanese. Okinawa was not a popular meeting place for future 52-Charlie cadets. Pierson served off Okinawa on the *Iowa* and was hit by a shell in the number two turret. Vogel was on the *Wesleyan* and almost got blown out of the water, and Max Hanson watched a Japanese torpedo hit the side of his destroyer and bounce off.

After the war ended, Pierson returned to high school to get his diploma. But he was hooked. He wanted to spend his life in the service. He applied for aviation cadets and was accepted into the class of 52-Charlie in Greenville, finished his training in B-25s at Reese and B-29s at Randolph. He flew thirty combat missions over Korea from Yakota, Japan, with virtually nothing to tell his grandchildren about. His first combat mission was like his last, uneventful. Take off, fly to the target, drop bombs, turn around and return to base for three days of R & R. Sounds routine, but when the enemy is shooting live ammunition at you and you see bursts of ack-ack near your plane, when there are MiGs in the area fully intent on shooting you down, it is a bit more than routine.

Pierson's experiences in Korea were just the beginning of a remarkable career. When the Korean War ended, he served as aide-de-camp to the commanding general of the Japanese Air Defense Force. He was assigned to the Strategic Air Command, flying nuclear-loaded B-52s and B-47s.

Pierson spent four years flying combat in Vietnam. He flew a thousand sorties in four different aircraft: the A-37 and F-5 air-to-ground jet fighters, the OB 10 forward air control small reciprocal engine spotter, and the huge and very slow C-123 troop carrier. In his four years of combat, he landed many aircraft that had been riddled by enemy fire. When you fly air-to-ground support missions, you fly so low that a road apple could down you. But the most frightening mission he flew was in the C-123. He was flying over the Michelin rubber plantation in Vietnam when his plane was hit by ground fire. Two soldiers in the rear of his aircraft were killed and the linkage to his ailerons was severed, making his control yoke virtually useless. The only way he could raise or lower a wing or turn was by alternating power from one engine to another. Not only did Pierson manage to bring his plane safely back to the base, but he landed the aircraft without further incident.

Pierson served as an operations advisor to the Vietnamese Air

Force and the Royal Thailand Air Force. In between volunteer combat tours in Vietnam, he instructed student pilots in T-38s at Craig and Reese Air Force bases. During his career, he accumulated more than 10,000 flying hours in planes with one, two, four, six, and eight engines. As commander of the "Nail" Forward Air Controllers, he was the last to fly out of Cambodia in August of 1973. Pierson was a graduate of three institutions and an associate professor at four universities. He was a founder and president of Top Gun and Formation Leadership seminars and a consultant to American Airlines.

Howard Pierson collected hardware, and, oh, what a collection he has! His combat decorations include the Airman Medal for Valor, three Distinguished Flying Crosses, three Bronze Stars, thirty-nine Air Medals, the Meritorious Service medal, the Vietnamese Gallantry Cross, and a host of lesser awards. And then to top it off, Pierson was named to the Air Commando Hall of Fame.

In 1979, thirty-five years after he watched his ship the *USS Iowa* take a shell off the coast of Okinawa, Howie Pierson retired with silver birds on his shoulders and a record that may never be equaled. Howie Pierson does indeed have something to tell his grandchildren.

Perfect Timing

Ralph Mackey the navigator

Some people were born on the right side of the clock. Ralph Mackey was one of those people. Most of the important crossroads in his life came at just the right time. In 1943, at the age of nineteen, Mackey received his wings as a bombardier in the Army Air Force. He was sent to England to fly combat in the venerable B-17. This was not a safe profession. It was rare for a crew to complete twenty-five combat missions, as the attrition rate was high. Nonetheless Ralph was young and the young were invulnerable. Besides, Ralph was a very close friend of Lady Luck, proof of which came on his twelfth mission to Munich, Germany. On that day a bombardier from another crew, a captain, approached Ralph and asked for a favor. The captain's mother was terminally ill in the States and he had been given an emergency leave to visit her. The captain had flown twenty-four missions and if he could fly just one more he would finish his tour and not have to return to England following his leave. But his crew was not scheduled to fly that day. So the captain approached Ralph Mackey for a favor. Would Ralph let him fly the mission in his place? Ralph decided it was a nice day to sit one out and agreed.

As the B-17s lined up for takeoff, the squadron commander ran up to Mackey in the mess hall and ordered him to get his parachute. A bombardier on one of the other 17s was sick and a replacement was needed, so Mackey flew the Munich mission after all but not with his regular crew.

The wing was escorted to the target that day by P-51s. They encountered little resistance from the Luftwaffe, but when they reached the IP, ground fire erupted. Black puffs of exploding flak dotted the sky like spots on a leopard. The plane that Ralph was flying in was cruising at 32,000 feet and right below him was the plane he normally flew. They turned over the target, their bomb bay doors opened, and their run commenced. Just then the plane carrying Mackey's regular crew was critically hit by flak. As Ralph watched, it slowly rolled onto its back and began a lethal dive to the earth. Ralph counted three chutes, though six men actually made it out of the stricken aircraft. Five members of Mackey's crew were killed that day. The other six members were captured and spent the rest of the war in a POW camp, including the captain who had replaced Ralph.

The ball turret gunner on that plane had the most miraculous escape. When the plane was hit the hydraulic system failed. The turret gunner's chute was in the belly of the aircraft. He had to turn the turret by hand until he could open the trapdoor into the plane. There he gathered his chute, closed the hatch, and by hand turned the turret until the trapdoor faced downward. He opened the hatch one more time and fell free, while the burning plane headed in a slow spin towards the earth.

Were it not for a very sick lady, Mackey would have been on that plane and his fate unknown.

Mackey's first eleven missions in WW II weren't exactly joy rides, either. On one, his plane flew into a heavy flak pattern and the con-

Ralph Mackey, second from the left in the back row, with the crew that was later shot down. The pilot, navigator, tail gunner, engineer, and radio operator were killed. The replacement bombardier and the others were captured on the ground.

cussion from an exploding antiaircraft shell ripped off part of the nose of his 17. That is where the bombardier sits. How he managed to survive that blast is still a mystery. Mackey and his entire crew made it back to England, but it was a very cold trip.

On another mission his troubles began even before he reached enemy territory. Everything seemed normal when suddenly there was a loud explosion and his oxygen mask blew several inches off his face before snapping back on his mouth with force. The Airplane Commander called the crew and asked if anyone knew the cause of the explosion. The tail gunner contritely explained that he had wanted a cigarette and when he lit a match, it exploded the oxygen system in the plane. The crew had to abort their mission and return to base. After they landed, every member of the crew emptied their pockets of cigarettes, covered the cigarettes with gasoline, and burned them. Mackey never smoked another cigarette from that day forward.

Mackey flew seven more combat missions in the B-17 before the war ended. He returned to the States with a lot of hardware and a lot to be thankful for.

When the Korean War began, Ralph Mackey was recalled. He decided that he had enough of bombers. They were too slow and too easy to hit. If he went to war again he wanted it to be in the seat of a fighter. He volunteered for cadets and was assigned to 52-C. Following graduation, Ralph was checked out in the F-51, the F-86, and the F-94. He assumed he was headed for the skies over Korea, but once again his timing was perfect. The Air Defense Command in the U.S. needed a replacement jet pilot and Ralph Mackey drew the long straw. Instead of dodging flak and MiG-15s in Korea, Mackey spent the balance of his time in the Air Force flying out of Selfridge AFB near Detroit, his biggest concern flying in foul weather. But the weather didn't shoot cannon shells. Ralph retired from the air force with more than fifteen hundred hours in the air, a fine relationship with Lady Luck, and a reputation for perfect timing.

The World Was His Office

Dale Christians and his co-pilot, Don Jordan, and navigator, Nobel Tibbets.

Dale Christians spent twenty-five years in the service and retired a lieutenant colonel. During his career, Christians flew F-84s, B-47s, and B-52s. He served in Korea and in Vietnam, where he flew forty-seven combat missions in the B-52. Many of those missions were flown near Hanoi, where ground-to-air missiles were in profusion and triple-A filled the sky. Christians was lucky. He never suffered any battle damage, but many in his group were less fortunate.

In 1959, Christians' crew won the most prestigious national competition in the Strategic Air Command based on air refueling, bombing, and navigation.

His favorite assignment was that of air attaché officer to the American embassy in Buenos Aires. Most of his time there was spent flying John Davis Lodge, the American ambassador, around Argentina. John was Henry Cabot's brother. Lodge believed he should be visible to all in Argentina, so he scheduled many flights to the interior.

When his tour of duty in Argentina was completed Christians tried to resign, but the Air Force had other plans. He held a critical AFSC, so off he went to Thailand, where he was assigned to Task Force Alpha, a high-security unit at Nakom Phanom.

The Air Force had inserted hundreds of FADSIDs (fighter aircraft delivered seismic intrusion devices) along the trails in North Vietnam. These units were dropped from low-flying planes or helicopters. They had spear points on one end and when they hit, they stuck in the ground. They looked like saplings but emitted an electronic signal when someone even tiptoed over the adjoining area. They were called McNamara's trees. Christians and his group of twenty officers were

Christians and his crew won the SAC bombing competition in 1959. Quite an honor. Quite a pilot.

responsible for analyzing what they heard. Their findings allowed the Air Force to pinpoint enemy movement and help determine where the enemy would strike next.

But the assignment that Dale enjoyed most was the Defense Intelligence Agency in the Pentagon. There everything that happened in the world came through his unit and he was responsible for getting that information to the Joint Chiefs of Staff.

Dale Christians made a career flying fighters and bombers in the U.S. and Vietnam, working with the heavy breathers, and performing cloak-and-dagger work inside and outside our country. A very exciting agenda.

Epilogue

After my combat tour I was transferred to the Strategic Air Command at Walker AFB in Roswell, New Mexico. I would spend the next two years there preparing for World War III should that come about. I was trained in the B-50 and assigned a target in China. Each month I spent at least three hours studying the flight plan to that target. At least once a month I was required to do an insert of a live atomic core into a bomb in my plane while flying at thirty thousand feet. I became proficient in air refueling at night and in new navigational techniques. At least once a month an alert was called and I would fly a mission of twenty-four hours or so, air refueling at least twice during the flight.

Once a year our entire squadron was sent on a three-month tem-

The B-50, a 29 with bigger engines, wing tanks, and a few other luxury options.

porary duty assignment. My first TDY took me to Guam and while I was there I had to fly our B-50 to Okinawa to avoid a hurricane that hit the island. That was quite a flight. We flew into the eye of the hurricane and out the other side. Sheets of rain covered the windscreen, St. Elmo's fire danced up and down our wings, lightning bristled all about, and the turbulence rattled the equipment inside.

The three months passed quickly and it was time to return to Roswell. Our flight plan took us to Quajelain for refueling and then on to Hawaii, where we arrived at midnight. I called in for landing instructions and was cleared into the pattern, and that's when I met my Mississippi River for the second time. As I turned onto final, the tower called, "Plane on final approach, identify yourself." I reminded the tower that I had just received clearance from them moments earlier.

"Plane on final approach, are you looking for Hickam by any chance? If so, you got the wrong runway, this is Clark field."

My God, was my face red! I broke out of the pattern and found Hickam immediately. We landed, went through customs, and went to bed. The next afternoon we took off for San Francisco.

Just before we left Guam, I saw a John Wayne movie about a commercial airliner, entitled *The High and the Mighty.* In the movie, upon reaching the point-of-no-return from Hawaii to San Francisco an engine falls from its mounting and it is touch and go all the way to 'Frisco. It was prophetic.

As we droned on towards California the mantle of darkness spread slowly over the endless ocean. The plane was on automatic pilot. There wasn't any turbulence; it was a perfect night for flying. Most of the members of the crew were asleep. I was listening to the musical theme from *The High and the Mighty,* which was being played on Armed Forces Radio. That should have told me something.

The navigator stuck his head around the gun turret and announced, "We have just passed the point-of-no-return." That meant we were midway between California and Hawaii, at the furthest point from land. I could hear the glasses rattling in John Wayne's aircraft and see the frightened expression on the stewardess' face.

Wham!!! My plane leaped forward and went into a steep dive. The automatic pilot couldn't hold the aircraft. I tried to pull the column back but was unable to right the ship.

The altimeter was a clock gone mad, unwinding: 25,000, 22,000, 20,000,15,000, 10,000—

I screamed at the flight engineer, but he didn't answer. It was a moonless night, black as pitch. I was not looking forward to an ocean landing. Landing hell, we would hit the water nose first. We lost about fifteen thousand feet within two minutes.

Finally, with both pilots pulling on the yoke, we were able to level the plane. We had just broken through 5000 feet, having lost 20,000 feet in a matter of minutes.

When we had regained control of the aircraft, the flight engineer told us the cause of our near disaster. He'd been using a gang plate to adjust the cowl-head temperatures on all the engines at once rather than adjusting them individually. The flaps stuck in the fully open position, creating so much drag it was impossible to fly the plane. Once the cowlings were back in trim, we regained our altitude and returned the plane to automatic pilot. I switched off Armed Forces Radio. I had had quite enough music for the night.

In the spring of 1954, my base commander honored me by selecting me to represent Walker AFB at the prestigious War College in Montgomery, Alabama. It was the most concentrated thirteen weeks I ever spent. Thirteen weeks of classes, plus lectures, war games and athletics, flying, and team meetings. An excellent education.

In May of 1955 I was separated from the service. As I drove through the gates at Walker AFB, for the first time in five years I was not saluted by the MPs. It was a sad moment.

We are told that a war ends when an armistice is signed. That is not true. A war never ends. Fifty years after an armistice was signed in Panmunjom, we are still learning things about that "police action." We are still staring across a DMZ and the North Koreans are still rattling their sabers. We have buried so many of our most valuable assets, young men and women who gave the ultimate sacrifice in Korea, Vietnam, Sarajevo, Afghanistan, Iraq, and in countless other cities and countries throughout the world. Fifty years does not dull the memory of these extraordinary people, and nothing will until we too are added to the HONOR FLIGHT that holds so many of our classmates.

I have repeated some of the stories of the pilots who graduated in the class of 52-Charlie. There are hundreds more. Many of those stories died in the skies over a small Asian peninsula or in prison camps in China and Russia. The stories of 52-Charlie are stories of bravery and sacrifice. They are the stories of a group of men dedicated to their country and to each other. Korea has been called the "forgotten war." It is not. As long as there's a Hasler or a Savage or a Griffith or a Fuller or a Spaulding or a Tudor regardless of generation, the Korean War will live. And the stories of 52-Charlie will be told and retold.

Printed in the United States
215709BV00002B/5/P

9 781604 942040